CELL PHONE LOCATION EVIDENCE FOR LEGAL PROFESSIONALS

CELL PHONE LOCATION EVIDENCE FOR LEGAL PROFESSIONALS

Understanding Cell Phone Location
Evidence from the Warrant
to the Courtroom

LARRY DANIEL

Principal Consultant
Guardian Digital Forensics, An Envista Forensics Company

ACADEMIC PRESS

An imprint of Elsevier

Academic Press is an imprint of Elsevier
125 London Wall, London EC2Y 5AS, United Kingdom
525 B Street, Suite 1800, San Diego, CA 92101-4495, United States
50 Hampshire Street, 5th Floor, Cambridge, MA 02139, United States
The Boulevard, Langford Lane, Kidlington, Oxford OX5 1GB, United Kingdom

Notices
Knowledge and best practice in this field are constantly changing. As new research and experience broaden our
understanding, changes in research methods, professional practices, or medical treatment may become necessary.

Practitioners and researchers must always rely on their own experience and knowledge in evaluating and using any
information, methods, compounds, or experiments described herein. In using such information or methods they
should be mindful of their own safety and the safety of others, including parties for whom they have a professional
responsibility.

To the fullest extent of the law, neither the Publisher nor the authors, contributors, or editors, assume any liability
for any injury and/or damage to persons or property as a matter of products liability, negligence or otherwise, or
from any use or operation of any methods, products, instructions, or ideas contained in the material herein.

British Library Cataloguing-in-Publication Data
A catalogue record for this book is available from the British Library

Library of Congress Cataloging-in-Publication Data
A catalog record for this book is available from the Library of Congress

ISBN: 978-0-12-809397-9

For Information on all Academic Press publications
visit our website at https://www.elsevier.com/books-and-journals

Working together
to grow libraries in
developing countries

www.elsevier.com • www.bookaid.org

Publisher: Sara Tenney
Acquisition Editor: Elizabeth Brown
Editorial Project Manager: Anna Valutkevich
Senior Production Project Manager: Priya Kumaraguruparan
Designer: Miles Hitchen

Typeset by MPS Limited, Chennai, India

For my wife, Erna, who has provided me with unwavering support and encouragement for the last 35 years; she has always been my anchor and safe harbor. She is the love of my life.

For my son, Lars, with whom I have had the great pleasure to work and write with over the last many years that he has been involved in digital forensics.

CONTENTS

List of Figures   xi
Author Bio   xiii
Foreword   xv
Preface   xvii
Acknowledgments   xix
About This Book   xxi

1. What is a Cell Phone?   1
Introduction   1
What is a Cell Phone?   2
Common Misconceptions   5
Summary   6

2. What is a Cell Tower?   7
Introduction   7
What About Special Events Where Towers Reach Capacity?   12
Cell Tower Sectors   13
Co-Location   14
Key Points About Cell Towers   16
Summary   16

3. A 20,000-foot View of the Wireless Telephone System   17
An Overview of the Wireless Telephone System   17
The Location Registers and Roaming   21
Summary   22

4. How Cell Phones Work in the Cellular Phone System   23
How Cell Phones Work in the Wireless System   23
Anatomy of a Cell Phone Call   26
Types of Phone Calls   27
Summary   28

5. How Does Cell Phone Location Work?   29
Introduction   30
How Does Cell Phone Location Work?   30
Summary   32

6. Call Detail Records—Origination, Business Purpose, and Contents   **33**
Introduction   33
Where Do Call Detail Records Originate?   34
Summary   40

7. How To Get Call Detail and Cell Tower Records   **41**
Introduction   41
Where to Obtain Call Detail Records   42
How to Request Call Detail Records and Cell Tower Lists   43
Obtaining Records From the Opposing Party   45
Summary   47

8. How Cell Phone Location Evidence is Presented in Court   **49**
Introduction   49
Summary   57

9. Issues With Using Call Detail Records for Location Purposes   **59**
Introduction   59
Call Detail Records   60
Summary   67

10. Drive Testing, What It Is, and How It Is Used as Evidence   **69**
Introduction   70
What is Drive Testing?   70
Drive Testing Data Collected   73
Drive Testing Methods   74
Drive Test Analysis   74
Drive Testing as Evidence   76
Summary   78

11. Per Call Measurement Data—Real Time Tool—Network Event Locations System Data   **79**
Introduction   80
What is "Precision Location" Data?   80
What Are Per Call Measurement Data, Real Time Tool, and Network Event Locations System?   80
Per Call Measurement Data   81
Real Time Tool   83
Network Event Locations System   85
Summary   88

12. Emergency 911 System   **89**
911 Wireless Services   90
Enhanced 911 Wireless Location Services   93
The Enhanced 911 System Overview   93
Location Technology   95
The Future of Enhanced 911   97
Tracking a Phone Using Enhanced 911   97
Summary   98
References   98

Index   *99*

LIST OF FIGURES

Figure 1.1	Standard cell phone	3
Figure 1.2	Cell phone and smart phone	3
Figure 1.3	Transmit and receive	4
Figure 2.1	A cell tower mounted on a tall tower structure	8
Figure 2.2	A cell tower disguised as a pine tree in North Carolina	9
Figure 2.3	A cell site mounted inside a billboard	9
Figure 2.4	A cell site mounted on top of a water tower	10
Figure 2.5	A cell site diagram showing the equipment that manages the cell phones connecting to the cell tower antennas	11
Figure 2.6	Each sector can cover 120°. But not always	13
Figure 2.7	A two sector tower covering a long highway	14
Figure 2.8	A three sector configuration showing the azimuth. In this case, the azimuth of zero equals due north	15
Figure 2.9	A cell tower with co-located antennas for three different companies	15
Figure 3.1	A cell site	19
Figure 3.2	Anatomy of the cellular system	20
Figure 3.3	Wireless telephone network	20
Figure 4.1	Cellular system showing the home location registry	24
Figure 4.2	The phone will connect to a tower within radio range of the phone	25
Figure 4.3	A cell phone to cell phone call	26
Figure 4.4	A land line phone calling a cell phone	26
Figure 4.5	The hand off area between two cell towers	28
Figure 4.6	As a phone travels along a road, it will switch to towers within range along the route	28
Figure 6.1	A Sprint call detail record example	37
Figure 6.2	AT&T call detail record example	39
Figure 7.1	Search.org home page	42
Figure 7.2	Search.org ISP list dropdown	43
Figure 8.1	Coverage radius with sectors	51
Figure 8.2	Parking lot at night	52
Figure 8.3	Idealized layout of a network (a) and theoretical service areas of three sectors located on the same mast (b)	52

Figure 8.4   Radio coverage infographic   53
Figure 8.5   Automated software output   54
Figure 8.6   Using a "standard" radius   55
Figure 8.7   A hand drawn coverage map   56
Figure 8.8   A map with known information from call detail records   56
              and tower records
Figure 9.1   Example propagation maps   64
Figure 9.2   Propagation map showing radio coverage overlap   65
Figure 9.3   Signal strength comparison test   65
Figure 9.4   Multipathing or Rayleigh fading   66
Figure 9.5   Cell reception issues in the real world   66
Figure 10.1   RANAdvisor drive test system for network planning,   73
              deployment, and maintenance
Figure 10.2   PCTEL's SeeHawk Engage Lite product   73
Figure 10.3   Drive test coverage map   76
Figure 10.4   Drive test best server points for an isolated cell sector   77
Figure 11.1   Per call measurement data analysis   84
Figure 12.1   Time difference of arrival   95
Figure 12.2   Angle of arrival   96

AUTHOR BIO

Larry began performing computer forensics in 2001 and has accumulated over 20,000 hours of experience working in the field of digital forensics.

He also holds numerous certifications in computer, cell phone, and GPS forensics including the Encase Certified Examiner (EnCE), Access Data Certified Examiner (ACE), Digital Forensics Certified Practitioner (DFCP), Blackthorn 2 Certified Examiner (BCE), the Access Data Mobile Examiner (AME), Certified Telecommunications Network Specialist (CTNS), Certified Wireless Analysis (CWA), and Certified Telecommunications Analyst (CTA).

Larry has provided computer and cellular phone and cellular tower technology in hundreds of criminal and civil cases. Additionally, he has qualified and testified as a computer forensic expert, a cellular phone forensics expert, a GPS forensics expert, and a cellular technology expert over 50 times in state and federal courts.

He is the co-author of the book, "Digital Forensics for Legal Professionals, Understanding Digital Evidence From the Warrant To the Courtroom" 2011, Syngress.

ACKNOWLEDGMENTS

- Sarah Rackley Olson, Forensic Resource Counsel, North Carolina Indigent Defense Services. Sarah has always been encouraging and willing to review proposals and outlines of my works.
- I also acknowledge Jerry Grant, my friend and fellow expert.

ABOUT THIS BOOK

Cell Phone Location Evidence for Legal Professionals is a guide, in plain language, for attorneys, students, the general public, and forensic professionals interested in the sources, methods, and evidence used to perform forensic data analysis of call detail records, real time ping records, and geo-location data obtained from cellular carriers and cell phones.

This book is not about the data that can be recovered from cell phones or other connected devices as that is a separate book altogether.

Throughout this book the author will refer to cell phone location evidence, cellular data analysis, or cell phone location forensics interchangeably as they all mean the same thing: The attempt to locate a phone's whereabouts using data obtained from cellular carriers or from the cellular device or phone.

This book is not intended to make the reader an expert in the area of cellular data analysis or cell phone location forensics, but it is intended to provide to working legal professionals and others with an interest in this field the information needed to understand what this type of evidence means, where it comes from, how it is analyzed and presented, and how it is used in various types of civil and criminal litigation.

Examples are provided throughout the book to help the reader to understand the evidence, how it is collected by the carriers, how to obtain evidence via subpoenas, and how it is analyzed and presented.

These case studies will show both correct and incorrect usage of cell phone location data as well and the common mistakes made by analysts.

CHAPTER ONE

What is a Cell Phone?

Contents

Introduction	1
What is a Cell Phone?	2
Cell phones come in two varieties: cell phones and smart phones	2
How does the cell phone work?	4
Common Misconceptions	5
Summary	6

Abstract

This chapter discusses what a cell phone is and how it communicates with the cellular network. As simple as the question sounds, while most people would say it is a telephone, most do not really know what a cell phone actually is. Also discussed in this chapter, what happens when the cell phone cannot communicate with the wireless telephone network and why? Also, common misconceptions about phone tracking are explained.

Keywords: Cell phone; smartphone; tower outage; cell tower

Information in this chapter:

- What a cell phone is?
- Cell phones and smart phones.

INTRODUCTION

Each time I am on the witness stand to testify about cell phones and location evidence, the first question I am normally asked is, "What is a cell phone?"

While this seems like a super simple and almost ridiculous question since nearly everyone has a cell phone, how could anyone not know what a cell phone is? But the truth is, most people do not know what a

Cell Phone Location Evidence for Legal Professionals.
DOI: http://dx.doi.org/10.1016/B978-0-12-809397-9.00001-8

1

car is, they just know they drive one. Ask just about anyone what a car actually is and you might be surprised to get an answer like, "A mode of transportation, or something you drive." You probably would not get any information regarding the type of engine, the rear differential ratio, or that it is powered by an internal combustion engine that uses explosions to push pistons by applying an electrical spark to gasoline vapor inside the piston cylinders.

WHAT IS A CELL PHONE?

So, what is a cell phone? In its basic form, a cell phone is a two-way radio. You could think of it as a walkie-talkie without the need to press the send button every time you want to say something.

When you dial a phone number using the keypad on the cell phone and press the send button, the phone uses a radio connection to a cell tower to place the phone call. The call then travels over wires from the cell tower radio antenna to the standard land line telephone system. I have had people tell me they thought the cell phone call would jump wirelessly from one cell tower to the next until it reached the phone that was being called. That is not the case.

Cell phones come in two varieties: cell phones and smart phones

Originally cell phones could do nothing more than make or receive telephone calls. When I got my first cell phone, it was so large it had to be installed in a vehicle. Later on, you could buy a "bag" phone that a person could carry around. This was also heavy and bulky. Once phones began to become more common, the phone itself would consist of a dial pad and some type of small display you could use to see what number you were dialing or what number was calling you. These old phones, called "bricks" were bulky and heavy. Once the "flip phone" was introduced, phones became stylish. Flip phones were inspired by the communicators used in the original Star Trek series. Beam me up Scotty! (Fig. 1.1).

Over time, a standard cell phone became more than just a telephone, it could handle voice calls and text messages. But in effect it was still just a standard cell phone.

Figure 1.1 Standard cell phone.

Figure 1.2 Cell phone and smart phone.

Once technology progressed to the point that a decent sized screen and a better keypad was available, the smart phone was introduced. A smartphone by definition, combines the cell phone capabilities of voice and texting with those of a handheld computer to also take and display pictures, movies and the ability to load and use all kinds of applications on the phone from navigation to word processing (Fig. 1.2).

How does the cell phone work?

For a cell phone to work, it has to have at least two types of radios built into the phone: a transmitter radio and a receiver radio. To make or receive a phone call, a cell phone must use two radio channels: a channel to send voice transmissions to the wireless telephone network and a channel to receive voice transmissions from the wireless phone network (Fig. 1.3).

Most everyone has at one time experienced a situation where while on a phone call, one person can no longer hear the other. This occurs when the cell phone can no longer maintain one of the two required radio channels. So if the transmission radio channel drops connection, you can hear (receive) but you cannot talk (transmit).

As long as the cell phone is within radio range of a cell tower, the phone can make or receive phone calls using the wireless telephone system. There are rare exceptions where even if the phone is within range of a cell tower, it would not be able to make or receive phone calls. Some of these exceptions are as follows:

1. The cell towers within range are at capacity. When this occurs it is normally in conjunction with a special event such as a sporting event, a weather event or some other event that would have too many people trying to use the cell towers in the area at once. This is not a normal occurrence and in fact is quite rare. We all know this from using our cell phones on a regular basis and we know how rare it is to occur. How often are you in an area where you have a good signal, but you cannot make a phone call? It is easy to tell when this happens as you

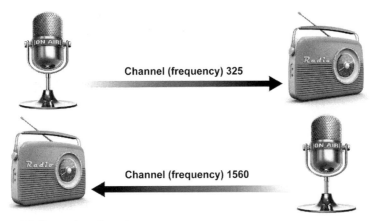

Figure 1.3 Transmit and receive.

will typically get a message from the cell phone company telling you that all circuits are busy. Or you may get a fast busy tone when you try to make a phone call. When this happens it is not a question of signal strength, that is how many bars you have, but a question of capacity, that is how many radio channels the tower has to work with and how many are occupied when you try to make your phone call.

2. The phone is in an area with no service from its company. No phone company has 100% coverage in all areas. Especially in rural areas where cell towers are far apart, or the terrain makes it difficult to provide coverage, such as in very mountainous areas or in areas with large inaccessible locations such as the Everglades. Also, bear in mind that your phone can only connect to cell towers operated by your phone company; or cell towers owned by other companies that your phone company has a roaming agreement with.

3. The only cell tower within range of the phone is out of service. This would be a very rare occasion since the cell phone companies monitor all of the cell towers in their networks 24 hours a day, 7 days a week. When a cell tower goes out of service, technicians are dispatched very quickly to get the cell tower back on line as having a cell tower out of service creates problems for the cell phone company and can generate a large number of complaints.

COMMON MISCONCEPTIONS

Many people believe that your phone is tracking you at all times. While your phone, if it has a GPS chip, does "know" where you are at all times, that information is not recorded by the wireless telephone company that provides your cell service.

Another popular myth is that the wireless telephone company can turn on a cell phone that is turned off. This is impossible simply because a cell phone that is turned off is not in communication with the wireless telephone network in any way. There is no secret signal that can be sent to turn on a cell phone that is turned off.

The same is true if a cell phone is placed into airplane mode. Airplane mode turns off all of the radios in the phone, preventing the cell phone or the wireless telephone company from making any kind of connection between the phone and the network.

Finally, if the battery dies on a cell phone, the phone is turned off or if the phone is placed into airplane mode, or the phone is in an area where there is no signal, there is nothing the wireless telephone company can do to determine why the cell phone is not communicating with the wireless telephone network.

If the phone is not communicating with the wireless telephone network, no records about the location of the phone can be created and stored at the wireless telephone company.

SUMMARY

In this chapter we looked at the characteristics of standard cell phones versus smart phones. We also dispelled the myth that cell phone companies record the locations of very cell phone in their network at all times and talked about what happens when the cell phone cannot communicate with the wireless telephone network.

CHAPTER TWO

What is a Cell Tower?

Contents

Introduction	7
What About Special Events Where Towers Reach Capacity?	12
Cell Tower Sectors	13
Co-Location	14
Key Points About Cell Towers	16
Summary	16

Abstract

This chapter describes some of the types and configurations of cell towers for wireless telephone systems. The chapter includes details of what a cell tower is, the equipment that is located within the cell tower site, and how the radio antennae can be configured to cover a specific area. The idea of beam width is introduced along with cell tower sectors and how they work.

Keywords: Cell tower; cell site; sector; omnidirectional; radio; tower capacity

Information in this chapter:

- Cell towers.
- Cell sites.
- Tower capacity.
- Antenna beam widths.

INTRODUCTION

When most of us think about the wireless telephone system, if we think about it at all, cell towers would probably come to mind. This is because cell towers are typically the only visible part of the wireless telephone system. However, some cell towers or more appropriately, cell sites, are not visible at all. In this chapter, you will learn about cell towers and the different configurations, and how capacity is calculated to

Cell Phone Location Evidence for Legal Professionals.
DOI: http://dx.doi.org/10.1016/B978-0-12-809397-9.00002-X

determine where to place cell towers or when new cell towers are needed (Figs. 2.1−2.4).

Since cell towers tend to be unsightly, some governing bodies attempt to reduce their visible presence by having the wireless telephone company disguise them as trees or cacti or some other naturally occurring object.

Cell towers can also be disguised somewhat by hiding them in other objects.

While it is interesting to review the ways cell towers are hidden, it is more important to discuss how they work and how they are configured.

A cell tower is more technically and correctly referred to as a cell site.

Cell sites contain radio antennas mounted on a structure, a piece of equipment to manage the mobile stations (cell phones) in the area, and in most cases, a battery backup system or emergency generator. You may have seen the television commercial "Verizon | A better network as explained by New Orleans Saint's backup quarterback Luke McCown." In the commercial he talks about how the backups just need a chance to prove themselves in the Verizon network. The commercial is being used to show that Verizon has great reliability for service since it has the backup generators in the system that assure that in the event of a power

Figure 2.1 A cell tower mounted on a tall tower structure. Photo by Larry Daniel.

Figure 2.2 A cell tower disguised as a pine tree in North Carolina. Photo by Larry Daniel.

Figure 2.3 A cell site mounted inside a billboard. Photo by Larry Daniel.

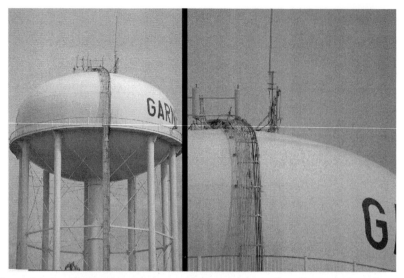

Figure 2.4 A cell site mounted on top of a water tower. Photo by Larry Daniel.

outage, the system will be up and operational to serve Verizon's customers.

Cell sites include not only the visible cell tower you can see, they also include special equipment to handle the radio signals in the area, process the phone calls, data transmissions, and text messages. See Fig. 2.2. This equipment also provides management of cell phone connections to the system, and acts as a way for the phones in the area to connect or disconnect as they enteror leave the radio range of that particular cell site (Fig. 2.5).

Depending on the type of radio network in use by the wireless telephone company, the equipment might be called a base transceiver station (BTS) or a base station controller (BSC) in 3G networks. The purpose of the BTS is to manage the phones within the coverage area of the cell tower. In newer 4G systems, this piece of equipment is referred to as Enhanced Node B. A deeper discussion of 3G and 4G is found in Chapter 3, A 20,000-foot View of the Wireless Telephone System.

Rather than switching back and forth between the terms, I will refer to all cell sites as cell towers.

From the standpoint of how cell towers impact the way that evidence is gathered and eventually presented, it is important to understand how cell towers can be configured.

This leads to the discussion of why cell towers are placed as they are to provide wireless telephone service to a particular area.

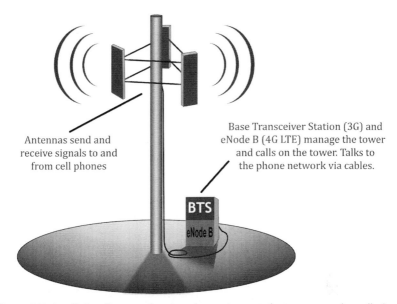

Figure 2.5 A cell site diagram showing the equipment that manages the cell phones connecting to the cell tower antennas.

Cell towers (sites) can only handle a limited number of calls. For this reason, cell towers are placed to cover a geographical area based on the maximum number of subscribers who are expected to attempt to make phone calls during a peak period of time.

To unpack that statement, let us look at this constructed example, not based on any information directly from a wireless phone company; Along I-85 North moving through downtown Raleigh, NC, the wireless phone company expects that there will be 1000 of their subscribers in a mile-long stretch of that highway during peak rush hour times. They would then estimate that 70% of those subscribers would need to connect to a cell tower because they start a call, receive an incoming call, or are already on a call and need to hand off to the cell tower.

So now we know that the engineers are estimating the need to handle a peak load of 700 phone calls at peak times along a 1-mile stretch of highway.

Now the second part of the analysis is that each cell tower can only handle 500 phone calls at a time. Remember that cell towers have a limited capacity to handle calls.

In addition to having a total capacity for 500 phone calls, some of that capacity has to be reserved for subscribers entering the coverage of the cell site. About 20% is reserved for that purpose. That leaves the ability to handle 400 active phone calls per tower with 100 spaces left over for people entering the coverage area of the cell tower while already on a call.

This means that in order to provide service to all 700 subscribers, the wireless telephone company will need to place two cell towers (700/ 2 = 350) with a capacity of 400 calls each. Otherwise, some subscribers will NOT be able to make are receive a call, or will have calls in progress dropped. This would not make the subscribers happy and they would eventually seek to find a carrier with more consistent coverage.

WHAT ABOUT SPECIAL EVENTS WHERE TOWERS REACH CAPACITY?

When a cell tower reaches capacity, the most likely scenario is that subscribers will not be able to make new phone calls. It is easy to tell when a tower is at capacity if you are the person using the cell phone because when you try to make a new phone call, you will not be able to get a channel. This is not the same thing as not having coverage. You can have a full set of bars in the radio strength meter of your phone. The issue is that the cell site does not have any radio channels free to handle your call. When this happens you may hear a fast busy signal, or you may get a message that the call failed, or you may hear a message that all circuits are busy.

In some instances, your call may be picked up or routed to another cell tower in the area, but this is impossible to prove from an evidentiary standpoint. If at the time a cell tower is at capacity and you are in an area where you are in the coverage footprint of more than one cell tower (the hand off area), then your call can be picked up by a tower that still has available capacity.

These occurrences are rare, and from an evidence standpoint, almost impossible to prove that a tower was at capacity at a particular time.

Each cell tower is configured to cover a specific area. There is no such thing as a "standard" or "average" coverage range for a cell tower.

When evidence is presented in the form of maps created based on call detail records, the expert should not include diagrams that purport to show the specific coverage area of a cell tower unless those maps are generated by the wireless telephone company.

CELL TOWER SECTORS

Each cell tower can have 0—6 sectors or sets of radio antennas. Most cell towers are configured to have three sectors. What this means is that a cell tower can have one radio antenna that covers a 360° range or the tower can have two or more radio antennas that cover some portion of the 360° circle.

Cell towers with zero sectors are called omnidirectional towers. Think of this kind of tower as being like a bare light bulb that shines in all directions at once.

However, for practical reasons of being able to better manage their networks, wireless telephone companies tend to primarily use three sector towers. The simplest way to think of a three sector tower is to visualize the peace sign. A circle divided equally into three wedges.

In cell tower parlance, that would be a 360° coverage area divided into three 120° wedges. See Fig. 2.6. I am using wedges as a convenience here. Radio waves emanating from a sector antenna DO NOT form a pie shaped wedge or a perfect circle. This will be discussed in detail in later chapters.

It is important to note that even though most of the time cell towers are configured as having three sets of radio antennas pointing outward 120° apart, this is not always the case. A three sector cell tower can also

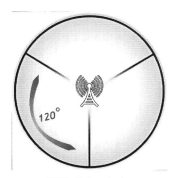

Figure 2.6 Each sector can cover 120°. But not always.

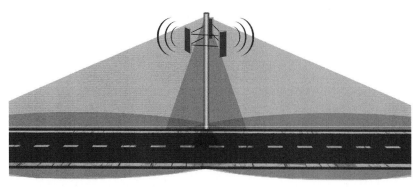

Figure 2.7 A two sector tower covering a long highway.

have radio antennas that do not equally divide the cell towers into three equal parts.

While a three sector cell tower is the most common configuration, cell towers with more or less sectors exist. For instance, a two sector tower may be used to cover a long stretch of highway in a remote area. When this occurs, the radio beam from the antenna may be narrower than 120° to make the beam go further. This is referred to as the beamwidth. In cases where there is a large, dense population of subscribers as will be found in major metropolitan areas, some cell towers will have six sectors, basically doubling the call capacity of the cell tower. Where a cell tower has more than three sectors, they may be configured with a narrower beamwidth such as six 60° wide sectors (Fig. 2.7).

Each sector is designated by a number and or name. The reason for this is that in some systems, the sectors are numbered starting with number 1 and in other systems the sectors are numbered starting with number 2. One way to avoid confusion is to use the universal names for the sectors: Alpha, Beta, and Gamma. The azimuth of a sector is the compass direction toward which the radio antennas are pointed. For instance, an azimuth of 0° would have the radio antenna pointing due north. An azimuth of 120° would point southeast (Fig. 2.8).

CO-LOCATION

Since it is expensive and difficult to erect new cell towers in populated areas, where cell towers are needed the most, many cell towers will house

Cell tower sectors
Sector layout and azimuth

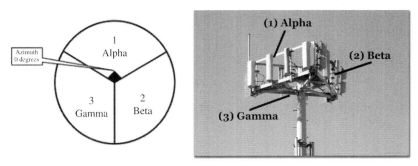

Figure 2.8 A three sector configuration showing the azimuth. In this case, the azimuth of zero equals due north.

Figure 2.9 A cell tower with co-located antennas for three different companies.

radio antennas for multiple companies. The cell tower in Fig. 2.9 has three sets of antennas, each belonging to a different wireless telephone company.

Key takeaways from this chapter are:

1. Cell towers do not have an "average" coverage area.
2. Cell towers can have 0−6 sectors.
3. A cell phone company can mount more than one set of antennas on a tower to provide greater coverage to the same area.

4. Radio waves to do not form perfect circles or "pie" wedges.
5. A cell tower can hold radio antennas for more than one wireless telephone company.

KEY POINTS ABOUT CELL TOWERS

1. Cellular networks in urban and suburban areas are designed for overlapping coverage, in other words multiple cell sites can cover the same geographic area. Cell site sectors are engineered intentionally with overlapping coverage between its own sectors as well as sectors of adjacent neighboring sites.
2. Antenna beam widths of 60° (six sector), 120° (three sectors), 180° (two sector), and 360° (omnidirectional) can all exist in the same local area depending on the needs of the wireless telephone company to provide cellular radio coverage. Directional antenna beam widths as a rule do not have distinct cutoffs, instead have gradual diminishing signal strength outside their designed beamwidth. This means that sectors that are beside one another overlap each other to a slight degree.
3. Distributed antenna systems (DAS): these are becoming very commonplace inside industrial complexes and large office buildings. Basically a cellular signal repeater with a directional antenna, pointing at a nearby cell site sector, and rebroadcasting signal within the building confines. (FYI—The metallic window tinting on modern windows effectively blocks most cellular signals from getting inside). It is helpful to understand DAS, as it can make a cell phone appear as if it is in one location when it is really in another.

SUMMARY

In this chapter we looked at some of the types and configuration of cell towers. We learned what a cell tower is, the equipment that is located in a cell tower site, and how the radios can be configured to cover a specific area. The idea of bandwidth was introduced along with the idea of sectors and how they work.

CHAPTER THREE

A 20,000-foot View of the Wireless Telephone System

Contents

An Overview of the Wireless Telephone System 17
The Location Registers and Roaming 21
Summary 22

Abstract

The wireless telephone or cellular phone system is part of the regular wired telephone system also known as the plain old telephone system (POTS) which provides the public telephone system we all use every day.

The wireless telephone system is made up of equipment that has been added to the POTS network to accommodate wireless voice and data calls.

The system is made up of cell sites (remote buildings with cellular radio equipment and antennas on towers), mobile switching centers, radio network controllers, or base station controllers and two databases called the home location register and the visitor location register. These network elements connect to the wired telephone system to provide wireless telecommunications capability to the wired telephone system.

Keywords: Cell site; cell tower; base transceiver station; base station controller; HLR; home location register; VLR; visitor location register; roaming; wireline; wireless

Information in this chapter:

- An overview of the wireless telephone system.
- The home and visitor location registers.
- Roaming.

AN OVERVIEW OF THE WIRELESS TELEPHONE SYSTEM

The wireless telephone network or "cellular" phone system interfaces with the original wire line telephone companies that provide wired residential and business phone services, aka the plain old telephone system

Cell Phone Location Evidence for Legal Professionals.
DOI: http://dx.doi.org/10.1016/B978-0-12-809397-9.00003-1
17

(POTS), which provides the public telephone system we all use every day. A POTS home telephone line uses the old analog system originally invented by Alexander Graham Bell and has remained basically unchanged except for moving from manual switchboard operators to automated switching equipment.

Newer non-POTS technology provides high-speed digital communications lines such as integrated digital services network (ISDN), digital subscriber line (DSL), and fiber distributed data interface (FDDI). While ISDN and DSL both use existing copper wires in the network, FDDI uses fiber optic cable made from a high quality optical glass.

The wireless part of the system is the wireless equipment that has been added to the POTS network to accommodate wireless voice and data calls. Think of it like the wireless router or modem you add to your home internet connection to allow laptop computers to connect without running cables everywhere in the home.

The cell phone network is made up of cell towers or cell sites connected to the standard telephone land line network. This means that a cell phone can call another cell phone or can call a land line phone anywhere.

Most of us think of the wireless telephone system as just being cell towers, if we think about it at all.

A cell tower, or more correctly, a cell site, is one or more cellular radio antennas mounted on a tower and connected to a set of processing equipment called a base transceiver station (BTS) or in the newer 4G network, an eNode B. For the purpose of this book the more common term cell tower will be used to refer to cell sites unless a distinction must be made for clarity. At the base of every cell tower there is a BTS that processes and handles local radio communications with cellular phones in the radio coverage area of the tower Fig. 3.1 shows a cell tower with BTS.

The wireless part of the system is made up of cell towers, base transceiver stations, base station controllers (BSCs), and mobile switching centers (MSCs) or switches and the home location and visitor location registers (HLR and VLR) that all connect to the wired telephone system.

Cell towers come in all kinds of shapes, sizes, and locations. A cell site can be a set of antennas mounted on a physical tower, on a water tank, on the roof of a building, or mounted on the side of a building. Cell sites or towers can also be disguised or hidden in areas where local codes require that the cell site not be a visual blight on the landscape. In these

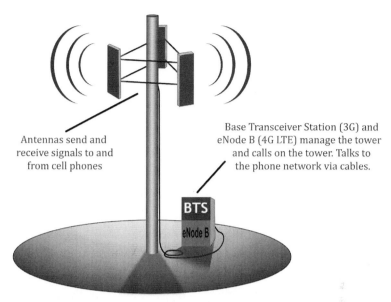

Antennas send and
receive signals to and
from cell phones

Base Transceiver Station (3G) and
eNode B (4G LTE) manage the tower
and calls on the tower. Talks to
the phone network via cables.

BTS

eNode B

Figure 3.1 A cell site.

cases, cell sites can look like giant artificial trees, a cactus, be hidden in a church steeple, or behind a billboard. (See Chapter 2: What is a Cell Tower? for more information about cell sites.)

There are also smaller mini-cells with omnidirectional antennas that cover a small 360° area. And then there are also microcells that are used to provide coverage in large venues such as sports arenas and large concert venues. Cellular repeaters, which are tiny cell sites, are placed in large glass and steel office buildings, shopping malls, and residential apartment buildings. These repeaters are also used in residential homes where there is a very weak cellular signal. A repeater can be obtained from the cellular phone company and connected to the internet connection in the home to provide cellular service.

At the base of every cell tower there is a BTS that processes and handles local radio communications with cellular phones in the radio coverage area of the tower.

The BTS is connected via broadband data service on a metallic or fiber optic terrestrial (land) network, microwave backhaul, or a combination of both; or via Ethernet cable to a BSC or radio network controller (RNC). The BSC/RNC manages several base transceiver stations as a group.

The BSCs are connected to a MSC or a mobile telephone switching office (MTSO) or "switch." For the purpose of this book, we will refer to switches. This grouping of cell towers connected to a switch makes up a location area. Each MSC typically manages the cell towers in a single market coverage area or location area. A market coverage area can be as small geographically as a few square miles in a city to hundreds of square miles in a rural area. See Fig. 3.2.

In a market area with a low population of subscribers, there will not be as many towers as there would be in a densely populated metropolitan area. This means that all of the cell towers in one or more small rural towns may be connected to a single market switch. In high density urban areas such as Washington, DC, or Chicago, IL, multiple switches are required to manage all of the cell towers needed in that city. A nutshell view is shown in Fig. 3.3.

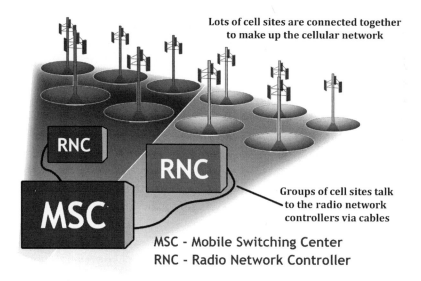

Figure 3.2 Anatomy of the cellular system.

Figure 3.3 Wireless telephone network.

THE LOCATION REGISTERS AND ROAMING

The Home Location Registry (HLR) is a database that permanently stores data about subscribers that have contracts with a wireless phone company. The HLR maintains subscriber-specific information such as the international mobile subscriber identifier (IMSI), international mobile equipment identifier (IMEI), and the current or last known location of the cell phone, roaming restrictions, and subscriber supplemental features. There is logically only one HLR in any given network, but generally speaking each network has multiple physical HLRs spread out across its network for performance and redundancy.

The Visitor Location Registry (VLR) is a database that contains the same type of information located on the HLR but only for subscribers roaming in its local location area from a different wireless carrier. When a phone goes into an area where there is no available service provided by its subscribed wireless carrier, the phone can roam on another carrier's cellular network, as long as the other carrier uses the same wireless technology. When this "foreign" phone enters the roaming area, it registers once with the HLR and then is added to the VLR. This is known as autonomous registration; the phone will register every so often so the system knows where the phone is located in the network.

This allows both the home network for the phone and the visited network to know that calls to this phone should be sent to the visited or foreign wireless carrier as long as the phone is roaming outside of its home network. From time to time the phone will perform "autonomous registration," so the network will know where the phone is in relation to cell towers close to the phone. The phone will also register a "kiss-off" message when the user powers the phone off intentionally. Just driving out of a service area, or the removal of the phone's battery will not transmit any kind of specific registration message.

A note about roaming; a phone can only roam on a network that uses the same technology as the phone's home network. This means that an AT&T phone that is a global system for mobile communication (GSM) only technology phone will typically not be able to roam on a Verizon network as Verizon uses Code division multiple access (CDMA) technology.

This would be a good time to introduce an important concept; the two competing technologies of the wireless telephone system: the GSM and the CDMA system. These two technologies make up the wireless telephone system in the United States. Worldwide, the GSM system is in use, where the CDMA system is primarily a US only technology. If you have ever wondered, this is why you cannot use certain cell phones in Europe or other countries that only support GSM phones. If your wireless telephone company is Verizon or Sprint, both CDMA technology companies, your phone would most likely only work in the United States and US territories unless it is an internally enabled phone that supports both CDMA and GSM technologies. Additionally, phones that are considered to be "world devices" are capable of using other technologies as long as the phone supports 4G LTE, Dual Band GSM, Quad Band GSM, and or Universal Mobile Telecommunications Service (UMTS) capabilities.

A phone that only has GSM technology built into the phone cannot use a CDMA technology network.

Additionally, when you are in an area where your telephone service provider does not have cell towers for coverage, your wireless telephone company must have a roaming agreement in place with your phone's home telephone company or your phone will not be allowed to use the network in the other telephone company's areas. So, for instance, if you are a Verizon customer and you are roaming in an area where Verizon does not have cell towers, you could use the Sprint network's towers as long as Sprint and Verizon have made an agreement to allow you to connect your Verizon cell phone to Sprint's cell towers. This is not something you decide or even know about, but the networks will know and will either allow your phone to make a connection or not.

SUMMARY

In this chapter we discussed the makeup of the wireless phone system and the various elements required for the wireless telephone system to work. We discussed roaming, and some of the types of cell sites used in the wireless networks.

We also discussed the HLR and VLR for subscribers' home and visiting networks. There was also a brief discussion of the various technologies used in the wireless phone system.

CHAPTER FOUR

How Cell Phones Work in the Cellular Phone System

Contents

How Cell Phones Work in the Wireless System   23
Anatomy of a Cell Phone Call   26
Types of Phone Calls   27
    Moving around—hand offs   27
Summary   28

Abstract

This chapter discusses the makeup of the wireless phone system and how cell phones work within that system. The different types of phone calls are described, as well as giving a detailed analysis of how cell phones work within the cellular phone system including communicating with other cell phones. An analysis is given of how the phone registers itself on the network and how it will act when it is moving (including the ability of the phone to switch to a different tower).

Keywords: Cell phone; cellular phone system; network; wireless; registration

Information in this chapter:

- Cell phone start up registration.
- Anatomy of a cell phone call.
- Types of phone calls.
- Hand offs.

HOW CELL PHONES WORK IN THE WIRELESS SYSTEM

A cell phone is basically a two-way radio that communicates with cell towers via radio signals. When a cell phone is turned on, it registers with the cellular system by contacting the network via a signaling/control and paging channel. This channel is used for a cell phone to announce its

Cell Phone Location Evidence for Legal Professionals.
DOI: http://dx.doi.org/10.1016/B978-0-12-809397-9.00004-3
23

presence to the network, in addition to accessing the system. During this registration process, the phone is identified in the home location register as a valid subscriber for the wireless carrier. Once the phone successfully registers with the network, it is allowed access to the network for its phone company, i.e. a Sprint phone is authorized to connect to Sprint's cell towers, and any features that are part of the subscriber's plan will be activated, such as data plans, text messaging, and voicemail. Fig. 4.1 shows a cell phone making a phone call with the elements of the system shown including the registration validation via the HLR (Home location register).

The registration process also allows the cellular system to know how to find the cell phone when the system needs to route a call to the phone. Bear in mind that this registration process is not part of a call detail record since this is not a billable transaction. In most cases, the data storage of these registration pings is only present for a few hours and are not recoverable after the fact.

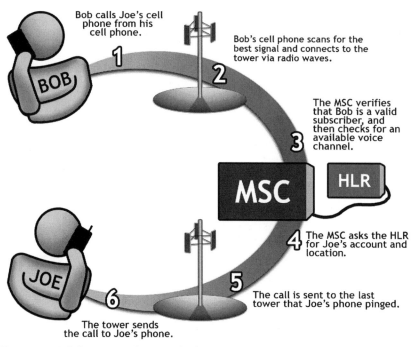

Figure 4.1 Cellular system showing the home location registry.

Figure 4.2 The phone will connect to a tower within radio range of the phone.

At this point, the cellular system knows the general location of the phone since the phone must connect to a cell tower within radio range of the phone to do this registration. The system then knows which local market area the phone is in and whether or not the phone is a "registered" phone. In other words, a registered phone is one that has an active account and can receive calls or make calls (Fig. 4.2).

There are differences in how cell phones register with, and how cell phones determine which tower will handle a call depending if the wireless telephone network is using Global System for Mobile Communication (GSM) or Code Division Multiple Access (CDMA) technology.

In a GSM network (AT&T and some others for example), once the phone is turned on and operating, it will periodically "ping" the tower with the strongest signal to maintain its registration so the system can locate it for incoming calls. Once the phone is on and active in the system, the phone will select a cell tower and then remain "camped" on that tower until the phone makes a decision to move to a tower with a higher quality radio signal. This type of tower selection is performed while the phone is in idle mode, meaning it is not in a phone call. Once the phone is in a call, the network will handle the tower selection if the phone must be moved to a different tower. This process is called a "hand off."

In CDMA networks (Sprint, Verizon, and others), I will note here that it is actually the phone that sends what are called PREPS (Pilot Reports), which are the signal strength messages of surrounding cell sites. The phone does this both while idle and during a call. The phone actually performs this housekeeping function, and tells the network what cell to send its voice/data traffic over, for optimum service.

ANATOMY OF A CELL PHONE CALL

This is a simplified description of how cell phones communicate using the cellular system. When a person dials a number on their cell phone those numbers and or symbols are stored in a "memory buffer" in the phone. Once the subscriber presses the "send" button, the phone will transmit those digits held in the memory buffer to the network in an attempt to place the call. The phone call will start its journey via the cell tower that the phone is currently "camped" on and will then travel along land lines since every cell tower is connected to the phone system via land lines. If the phone being called is another cellular phone, then the call will still traverse the phone system via land lines to the local market mobile switching center of the calling cell phone, to the central market switching center for the phone company, and then to the local market mobile switching center of the dialed phone. Then the call will be sent to the cell tower that the phone has registered with and finally to the phone itself. If the call is completed via Voice over Internet Protocol (VoIP), it is connected to the Public Switched Telephone Network (PSTN) at some point through a gateway or integrated media server (IMS).

Fig. 4.3 shows how the process works in a cell phone to cell phone call.

If the number dialed is a land line phone, then the call will traverse the land line telephone system and ring at the land line address. Fig. 4.4 shows the activity of a land line phone calling a cell phone. Ultimately, the cell phone will have to be located on the network and will connect to the network using a cell tower within radio range of that phone.

Figure 4.3 A cell phone to cell phone call.

Figure 4.4 A land line phone calling a cell phone.

TYPES OF PHONE CALLS

Once the call is started by the phone user, one of several things can happen:

1. *Completed call*: The called phone user answers the cell phone using the cell phone handset that was dialed. This is a completed call. The dialed digits and the phone number on the call detail record will in most cases match. However, if the user placing the call uses a speed dial number that would show up in the dialed digits column in place of the number dialed.

2. *Call attempt, no answer, caller gives up*: The person does not answer the cell phone and the person calling gives up by disconnecting the call. This is a call attempt.

3. *Routed call, no answer—the phone cannot be reached*: The phone number is a valid number but cannot be reached by any cell tower at that moment in time. The phone may be powered off, in airplane mode, or outside a service area. If the called phone subscription includes voicemail, this call may be routed to voicemail. The call may also just fail. This type of call would appear in the cell detail records, but would produce no valid cell tower information for the call. The reason is that a call that is routed by the network does not involve the phone in the process. Since the phone cannot be contacted, no valid cell tower information is available. There are exceptions to every rule and in some cases a routed call can create valid call location information. For instance, when a phone is using a third party voicemail system, the phone may place an outgoing call to that voicemail number, creating cell tower location data.

4. *Forwarded call*: The cellular number dialed has been forwarded to another number which can be another cell phone or a land line and the forwarded number is answered. The dialed digits and the answered phone number will not match since the dialed phone was answered by a different number. This is a completed call. There would not be any valid cell tower information stored in the call detail records for this call as the physical phone is not part of the call. The routing is handled by the network and the cell phone itself does not need to be powered on for forwarding to occur.

Moving around—hand offs

Once a phone is connected to a cell tower and in a phone call, it will remain on that cell tower as long as the network will allow it. Every phone works in harmony with the wireless phone network to attempt to

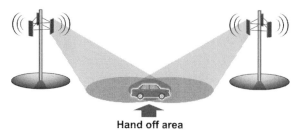

Hand off area

Figure 4.5 The hand off area between two cell towers.

Figure 4.6 As a phone travels along a road, it will switch to towers within range along the route.

provide the best quality phone call it can. However, as the phone moves around it will eventually get too far from the cell tower it is using to maintain good call quality and may be in danger of dropping the call all together. In the modern wireless phone system, the network equipment tells the phone when to switch towers and which tower to switch to in order to maintain the phone call in progress (Figs. 4.5 and 4.6).

Bear in mind that a phone does not need to travel very far for the phone to switch or hand off to a different tower. A hand off can occur even if the phone is stationary if it is within the hand off area between two or more cell towers.

SUMMARY

In this chapter we discussed the makeup of the wireless phone system and how cell phones work within the wireless system. Different types of phone calls were discussed along with how the phone registers itself on the network and how the phone will act when it is moving around causing the phone to "hand off" to a different tower.

CHAPTER FIVE

How Does Cell Phone Location Work?

Contents

Introduction   30
How Does Cell Phone Location Work?   30
Summary   32

Abstract

What is important to understand about location of a cellular phone or other cellular device is that the accuracy of the location is dependent on a number of factors, not the least of which is the ability of the analyst to properly interpret and present the data and the methods used to present the information. It is also important to understand some critical distinctions in terminology; knowing the cell tower and sector used by a cell phone does NOT provide a location for the phone. Performing a drive test does NOT provide the location of a phone. They only provide an estimated area where the cell phone could potentially be at the time the phone is connected to a cell tower.

There are more accurate methods for locating a cell phone than call detail records or drive testing, such as using the emergency 911 system to locate a phone.

This chapter will be a brief overview of how cell phone location works, how it is presented, and used in cases.

Keywords: CDR; Call detail record; 911; e911; RTT; PCMD; triangulation

Information in this chapter:

- Historical call detail records.
- Real-time data collection.
- Emergency 911 system.
- Drive testing.

Cell Phone Location Evidence for Legal Professionals.
DOI: http://dx.doi.org/10.1016/B978-0-12-809397-9.00005-5

INTRODUCTION

Any time you review evidence that proposes to show the location of a cell phone or other cellular device bear in mind that the accuracy of the location is dependent on a number of factors, not the least of which is the ability of the analyst to properly interpret and present the data as well as the methods used to present the information. It is also important to understand some critical distinctions in terminology; knowing the cell tower and sector used by a cell phone does NOT provide a location for the phone. It only provides an estimated area where the cell phone could potentially be when the phone is connected to a cell tower recorded in a call detail record.

There are more accurate methods for locating a cell phone than call detail records, such as using the emergency 911 (e911) system to locate a phone. However, using the e911 system must be done in real time and cannot be used to determine the location of a cell phone after the fact. This chapter is a preview of what is covered in the remainder of this book.

HOW DOES CELL PHONE LOCATION WORK?

There are several types of cell phone location data that can be collected and examined in order to more or less accurately determine the location of a cell phone. Each of the different types of data yields different results, some are more accurate than others for establishing the approximate location of a cell phone.

- Wireless telephone company data is collected in the form of *call detail records* for a particular phone along with a listing of the cell tower locations for that carrier. This kind of data may be referred to in legal briefs and opinions as historical CSLI (cell site location information). This data is then analyzed for the purpose of showing the cell towers and sectors used by a cell phone on a map. This provides the location of the cell tower the phone used, and does not give the location of the cell phone.

- Law enforcement may obtain a warrant to get near real-time call detail records for a phone. This is the same type of data contained in historical *call detail records* but is provided in near real time. This does not reveal the location of the phone. It is the same kind of analysis that would be done using historical call detail records and cell tower locations, but is performed in near real time. If the phone company is providing the cell towers and sectors being used by a cell phone very close to the time of the usage, it can give law enforcement information about the general location of a cell phone. For instance, if law enforcement agencies are trying to locate someone, this kind of analysis can tell them which side of town the phone is in or whether or not the phone has left the area and is traveling to a different city or state. However, bear in mind that this only reveals cell towers used by the phone for phone calls. This is not "pinging." If the phone does not have user activity in the form of phone calls, this type of analysis will not provide any location information.

- Cellular data can also come from various *real-time data collection* methods referred to as per call measurement data (PCMD), real-time tool (RTT), Network Event Location System (NELOS), and various other types of engineering data collected by the wireless carrier as the cell phone interacts with the network. This type of data is covered in detail in Chapter 11, PCMD−RTT−NELOS Data. These types of data come from engineering tools used by the carriers to check the health of their networks. They are not and never were designed to precisely locate a cell phone. Be wary as many experts will attempt to use this as precision location data.

- Cellular data in the form of "pings," which is real-time geo-location tracking of a cellular phone or other cellular device by activating the E911 system, which will then use either a network based or handset based method for locating the phone and will provide a location estimate generated via triangulation of the cell phone. This results in global positioning system (GPS) coordinates, latitude and longitude, of the estimated location of the phone itself. This method is more accurate than just using call detail records. However, it is not always accurate and typically will have a range of accuracy from a few meters to over a mile for each "ping." This type of data is covered in detail in Chapter 12, Emergency 911 System.

- In some cases, *drive testing* is employed to attempt to show that the analyst has more knowledge of where the phone might be than can be determined from call detail records alone. The process of drive testing will be covered to help the reader understand what drive testing is, how it is used in cases and how to properly interpret the drive testing maps. Drive testing is covered in detail in Chapter 10, Drive Testing, What It Is, and How It Is Used as Evidence.

SUMMARY

In this chapter we looked briefly at the most common methods of locating a phone: the analysis of historical call detail records, the e911 system, the real-time data collection, and the location data from applications and drive testing.

CHAPTER SIX

Call Detail Records—Origination, Business Purpose, and Contents

Contents

Introduction	33
Where Do Call Detail Records Originate?	34
Business purpose for maintaining call detail records or cell site location information	34
What data can be contained in a call detail record?	35
CDMA (Code division multiple access) network records	36
GSM (Global system for mobile communications) network records	36
Summary	40

Abstract

This chapter discusses where call detail records originate, how they are formed, what they contain, and how to read them.

Keywords: Call detail records; cell site location information; historical; switch

Information in this chapter:

- Call detail records.
- CSLI (cell site location information).
- Business purpose for call detail records.
- Issues to be aware of in reading call detail records.

INTRODUCTION

Call detail records are by far the most common type of evidence you will encounter in cases involving attempts to show the location of cell phones. The reason for this is call detail records are common to every wireless telephone company and they can be obtained after the fact, that

Cell Phone Location Evidence for Legal Professionals.
DOI: http://dx.doi.org/10.1016/B978-0-12-809397-9.00006-7

is historically. They are called historical cell site location information in many legal papers and briefings. Call detail records can also be obtained in near real time to assist in an ongoing investigation to determine the general location of a cell phone, that is, is the phone in a particular city, or area of a city. The business purposes for maintaining call detail records are also covered in this chapter.

WHERE DO CALL DETAIL RECORDS ORIGINATE?

In previous chapters we discussed the structure of the wireless telephone system. Parts of that structure are mobile switching centers or MSCs. A MSC or switch for short hand, controls a group of cell towers. As cell phones move around in the wireless network, the network traffic data for cell phone transactions are collected by switches.

The reason it is important to understand the concept of switches is this is where the data originates that will eventually become a call detail record.

As a phone uses the wireless telephone network all the transactions between the phone and the wireless telephone company are recorded at the switches. These transaction records include a great deal of information about the interaction of the cell phone with the wireless network in the form of voice calls, text messages and data transmissions. These transactions are stored in a database that can be queried later to extract data records. An important concept to understand is that call detail records are the result of a query that is performed in response to a request for information, be it via a warrant or a subpoena or even a request from the account holder. They are then compiled into a report format and provided to the requestor. What the requesting party receives is a report that is generated after the request for records is made.

Business purpose for maintaining call detail records or cell site location information

I had an attorney ask me not to long ago if there is an actual business purpose for the wireless phone companies to collect and store the information in call detail records. There are several business purposes for collecting and maintaining subscriber's interactions with a wireless phone company's network.

Proof of a service provided

One important and practical purpose for maintaining records of subscriber's interactions with the wireless phone company's network is to respond to questions and complaints that a subscriber might have regarding their wireless telephone service or account. For instance, if a customer wants to dispute their bill based on service interruptions or other service issues, the phone company can query the database and pull the records for the disputed time-period. This allows the company to show the customer that the service was provided.

A transaction record for financial accounting purposes

Even though the industry has moved away from detailed billing to flat rate plans in most cases, having the transaction records allows the wireless phone company to measure subscriber usage against the other flat rate plans. This lets the financial managers determine the profitability of flat rate plans versus metered or detailed billing plans. Also, the records collected allow for the analysis of network loading so that planning for the addition of new cell sites can be done to project future investment needs.

The records can also serve as a basis for cross company billing where the wireless phone company may have a roaming agreement with another wireless telephone company and need to pay or collect for usage on their network.

A technical picture of each transaction

Included in the data collected at the switch is information about which cell tower was used, how much time was used, whether a call was attempted and not completed, the channels used, and other technical information about the pilot signals, the technology for the call, that is 3G, EVDO (evolution data optimized), 4G, and so on. This type of data provides engineers information about the health of the network and the individual equipment in the network that is interacting with customers' cell phones and other connected devices like tablets with a wireless account with that provider.

What data can be contained in a call detail record?

The type of data that is collected and stored at the switch includes at least the IMEI (international mobile equipment identifier) of the physical cell phone, the IMSI (international mobile subscriber identifier) which identifies the user's account, the date and time of phone calls, data transmissions, and text messages. For each transaction with the network, the date and time will be recorded. For phone calls, a duration will be recorded showing the length of the phone call and in some cases the time it took for the phone call to connect to the dialed phone number.

There will also be codes that are collected that can be associated with various other information about the transaction such as the features used; voice mail, 3-way calling, call forwarding, and so on.

The keys pressed on the keypad of the phone will be recorded as dialed digits. The phone number for the receiving or dialed party may be shown. And the phone number of the phone that originated the call; the calling phone. There will also be an indication of the direction of the call or text message. Finally, depending in the type of network, there will be columns containing the switch NEID (network equipment identifier) or LAC (location area code) followed by the identifiers for the cell tower used to handle the start of the call.

For the two networks in use today, CDMA (code division multiple access) and GSM (global system for mobile communications), the records will look different.

CDMA (Code division multiple access) network records

CDMA network records will contain the switch identifier such as the NEID or Repoll number. CDMA records will then contain at a minimum the first cell tower that was used at the start of the phone call and may contain the last cell tower that the phone was connected to at the end of the phone call. CDMA records will not contain any cell tower information for text messages or data transmissions. Depending on the wireless telephone company and the way that they format their call detail records, the sector information for the cell tower that carried the phone call will be part of the cell tower identifier or will be contained in a separate column. For instance, Sprint typically includes the sector information as part of the cell tower identifier where Verizon puts the sector information and cell tower identifiers in separate columns. Bear in mind that each wireless telephone company formats their records differently. There is no standard format for call detail records. Fig. 6.1 shows a Sprint call detail record example.

GSM (Global system for mobile communications) network records

In GSM networks, the call detail records will contain the switch identifier, the cell tower identifier along with the latitude and longitude of the cell tower used. Depending on the wireless telephone company, the

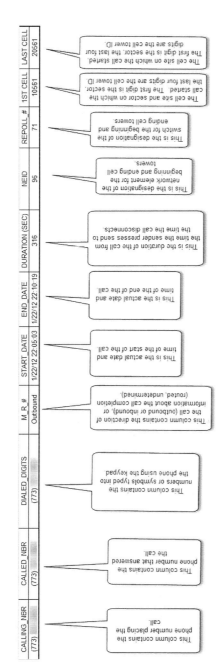

CALLING NBR	CALLED NBR	DIALED DIGITS	M.R #	START DATE	END DATE	DURATION (SEC)	NEID	REPOLL_#	1ST CELL	LAST CELL
(773)	(773)	(773)	Outbound	1/22/12 22:05:03	1/22/12 22:10:19	316	96	71	10561	20561

This column contains the phone number placing the call.

This column contains the phone number that answered the call.

This column contains the numbers or symbols typed into the phone using the keypad.

This column contains the direction of the call (outbound or inbound), or information about the call completion (routed, undetermined).

This is the actual date and time of the start of the call.

This is the actual date and time of the end of the call.

This is the duration of the call from the time the sender presses send to the time the call disconnects.

This is the designation of the network element for the beginning and ending cell towers.

This is the designation of the switch for the beginning and ending cell towers.

The cell site and sector on which the call started. The first digit is the sector, the last four digits are the cell tower ID.

The cell site on which the call started. The first digit is the sector, the last four digits are the cell tower ID.

Figure 6.1 A Sprint call detail record example.

azimuth or direction of the radio set (the sector), will be included in the call detail record as well.

However, the azimuth is not always included in every record, even if it appears in some of the records.

AT&T records may contain the starting cell tower information and additional cell towers that were used during the duration of the cell phone call. *Note:* In the GSM network, the first tower in the record is the tower that was chosen by the phone while it was in idle mode. Once the phone connects and is in a call, the network chooses the towers to use as needed by the network. This means that while the records may show connections to other towers during a call, those other tower locations are not valid for location purposes (Fig. 6.2).

Call detail records from other wireless telephone companies vary from the examples shown and may not resemble the examples at all.

Key issues of call detail records to be aware of are as follows:

1. Call detail records from different wireless telephone companies will contain a variety of information, not all of it useful to the analysis of historical call detail records. In fact, the variety of ways in which call detail records are formatted can be extremely confusing and should be interpreted by an expert or by the phone company providing the records.
2. Time stamps from different wireless phone companies vary. Some phone companies use local time at the switch, some use UTC (coordinated universal time), and some records are a combination. As an example, in one company's records, voice records are in local time, but text messages are always in Pacific Time, independent of the location of the phone.
3. The sector numbers for records in CDMA networks for Lucent switches are numbered differently from the sector numbers for Nortel or Ericsson switches and this must be accounted for in any analysis. In these cases, the cell tower records will not reflect this numbering difference.
4. The cell tower identifiers in some call detail records are based on the network using a feature called automatic roaming and the tower recorded is not chosen by the phone in those instances. In fact, the tower shown in the call detail records may be several miles away. This is an example unique to one company, and is not a general rule.

In Chapter 7, How to Get Call Detail and Cell Tower Records, you will find subpoena language to use in requesting call detail records and an explanation of why you are asking for certain pieces of information.

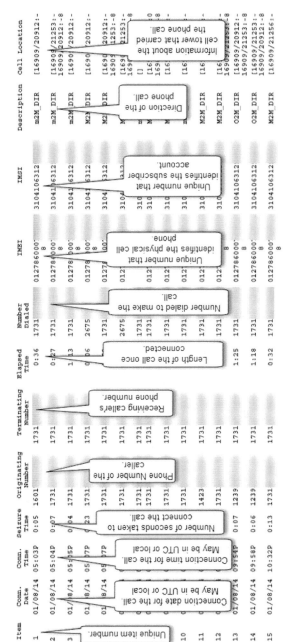

Figure 6.2 AT&T call detail record example.

SUMMARY

In this chapter, we discussed the origination of call detail records and how the data is collected at the switch in the networks. The business purpose for maintaining call detail records was covered along with the content of call detail records. Finally, issues with call detail records and how they vary from one wireless telephone company to another was also covered.

CHAPTER SEVEN

How To Get Call Detail and Cell Tower Records

Contents

Introduction   41
Where to Obtain Call Detail Records   42
How to Request Call Detail Records and Cell Tower Lists   43
Obtaining Records From the Opposing Party   45
    Getting cell tower records   46
Summary   47

Abstract

This chapter discusses how to ask for and how to get call detail records. Each of the line items you will be requesting from the wireless telephone company will be explained as to what it is and why you are asking for that particular piece of information.

It is critical that you obtain the most complete and accurate information for analysis and this chapter will assist you in that process.

Keywords: Call detail records; cell site location information; electronic formats; subpoena language; custodian of records

Information in this chapter:

- Call detail records.
- Subpoena language.
- Formats.
- Requests.

INTRODUCTION

Obtaining call detail records from the wireless telephone companies and from opposing counsel can be a challenge. This is because the

Cell Phone Location Evidence for Legal Professionals.
DOI: http://dx.doi.org/10.1016/B978-0-12-809397-9.00007-9

wireless telephone company, wants very specific information to provide the records and because middle men in the discovery process can impede your getting the right data in the right formats. When you want to obtain records from a wireless telephone company, you will need to ask for both call detail records, and for cell tower location records; and you will need to use very specific terminology to obtain what you want. This chapter will provide you with the detailed information you need in a form that will allow you to create subpoena requests to wireless telephone companies for call detail records and cell tower location lists. You will also learn about the process that occurs when wireless telephone companies respond to warrants or subpoenas from law enforcement agencies and how to make sure you get the same records they received.

WHERE TO OBTAIN CALL DETAIL RECORDS

To find the most up to date custodian of records information for each wireless telephone company, you can go to the website at www. search.org. The list for custodians is maintained by updates from law enforcement agencies who work with the wireless telephone companies on a regular basis and is called an ISP list on the website and can be found under the resources dropdown link (Figs. 7.1 and 7.2).

Figure 7.1 Search.org home page.

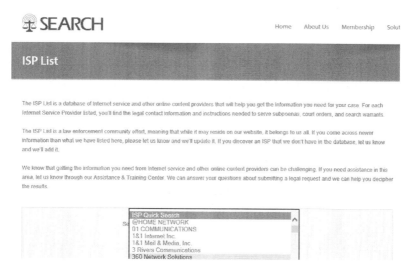

Figure 7.2 Search.org ISP list dropdown.

HOW TO REQUEST CALL DETAIL RECORDS AND CELL TOWER LISTS

The process is fairly straightforward for getting call detail records and cell tower lists from the various wireless companies. However, the additional information you should collect, such as maintenance or outage records, can be difficult or impossible to obtain. You will want to provide a detailed request to the wireless telephone company's subpoena compliance department to obtain records.

The requested information you will want to put into a subpoena or other type of request is:

Language for use in discovery motions and court orders for call detail records and cell tower locations. The items in **bold** *text should be edited to fit your particular case details.*

This is a request the following information be provided regarding cell phone communications in the form of historical call detail records and cell tower locations, for cell phone number(s) **000-000-0000** for the period of time between **00-00-2000** and **00-00-2000**.

All information including but not limited to:

1. Subscriber information for the above listed numbers, including financially responsible party, billing address, features and services, and equipment.

2. All call originations, call terminations, call attempts, voice and text message transactions, including push to talk, data communications, SMS and MMS communications, and voice communications, including the originating and receiving phone numbers or network IDs for all incoming and outgoing call transactions, data transactions, and push to talk sessions.

3. Records are to include the IMEI, IMSI, or other equipment or handset identification information for the target phone number.

4. All stored SMS content and MMS content when available.

5. Beginning and ending switch and cell site/tower identifiers for each call, SMS, MMS, and data transmission, including the location information, azimuth, and beam width for the tower and sector used for the call.

6. Registration and de-registration messages, kiss, or other hang up messages and information regarding the activity of the cell phone in the network.

7. A complete table of cell towers/cell site information for all cell towers/cell sites in the LAC, NEID, or service area, and/or for all switches used, active at the time period for the call detail records requested.
     This shall include:
     a. cell tower location information including latitude and longitude;
     b. cell tower/cell site designation information/identification numbers;
     c. information for each cell site sector including azimuth;
     d. equipment type used at the cell site, Lucent or Nortel, etc.;
     e. Note to At&T and T-Mobile: Even though the tower location information is in the call detail records, this subpoena also requests a list of cell tower locations with the latitude, longitude of each tower, the sector azimuth, and the beam width, if known, for the time period covered, in comma delimited or Excel format, for every tower referenced in the call detail records responsive to this subpoena.

8. A legend and definition for any and all abbreviations used in the reports provided.

9. An explanation of how to read the call detail records.

10. Specific information regarding the time stamps/time zones of the records.

11. Any precision location data such as PCMD, RTT or NELOS records for the time period requested.

Provide the following information regarding cell tower locations for the following areas containing cell towers actively in service between **August 1, 2014** to **August 31, 2014**.

For each LAC/NEID or switch that that is operational for a 25 mile radius of downtown **Albany, NY**.

Include the below cell tower information:

LAC/NEID/REPOLL/SWITCH NAME or ID

Tower number

Sector number

Latitude

Longitude

Sector azimuth

Horizontal beam width if known.

- Any records or information regarding cell towers that were undergoing maintenance, or were out of service the time period in this request.
- All responsive data is to be provided in both Adobe PDF format and Microsoft Excel format, .TXT, or .CSV format.

Please indicate in your response to this subpoena if there is any data loss due to the time difference between the date of the receipt of this subpoena and the time period requested, and if so, a detailed description of what data is not recoverable versus what data would be recoverable based on the carrier's retention period for call detail records.

Please respond to this subpoena via email to: **someone@youremail-address.com**

OBTAINING RECORDS FROM THE OPPOSING PARTY

In many cases you will be requesting records be provided to you as part of the discovery process. When this happens, you will want to make sure that you obtain everything that the wireless telephone company provided to opposing counsel. Bear in mind that when the wireless telephone companies respond to a court order, subpoena, or search warrant, they will normally provide the records in electronic format as an attachment to an email to the requestor. What you want to receive in discovery is the email and the attachments to the email that was sent to the requestor so that you get the exact same files the wireless telephone company provided.

The reason this is so important is that in many cases the telephone or call detail records that will be provided to you in discovery will be scanned copies of printed versions of the electronic documents. These scanned copies are not the electronic format you want as they do not allow you or your expert to efficiently analyze the records. In some cases, this will force your expert into hand keying records which is time consuming, prone to errors, and every expensive.

Also, with AT&T and T-Mobile, you will not receive a cell tower list since the cell tower locations are in the call detail record for each phone call. It is critical that your expert have access to the cell tower locations for all the towers for that wireless telephone company. You will in most instances have to request these tower locations separately via subpeona.

Law enforcement agencies can get access to a website that contains a database of cell tower locations maintained by the FBI. Each month, the wireless telephone companies provide an archive listing of cell towers to the FBI for inclusion in this database as part of their compliance with the Communications Assistance to Law Enforcement Act (CALEA). This allows the FBI and other law enforcement agencies to obtain cell tower listings for any carrier for any period of time. However, the list obtained in this manner will not typically be included in your discovery from the opposing counsel in criminal cases.

When you cannot get the cell tower listings from opposing counsel for whatever reason, then you will have to subpoena that information directly from the wireless telephone company. Bear in mind that some of the wireless telephone companies will be reluctant to provide cell tower locations or may even refuse to do so. In that case, you might want to pursue a court order to compel them to comply with your request.

Getting cell tower records

Technical language for your subpoena to obtain a list of cell tower locations that correspond to the date and time of the incident would include the following (be sure to replace the items in bold text with your particular details):

To Custodian of Records,

This is not a request for call detail records, but for the locations of cell towers only.

Provide the following information regarding cell tower locations for the following areas containing cell towers actively in service between **August 1, 2014** and **August 31, 2014**.

For a **15 mile radius of downtown Atlanta, Georgia**.
Include the below cell tower information:
LAC or NEID/REPOLL/SWITCH
LAC/NEID/REPOLL/SWITCH NAME or ID
Tower number
Sector number
Latitude
Longitude
Sector azimuth
Horizontal beam width if known.

- Records to be provided on CD or via email in Microsoft Excel format or as comma delimited text files (.txt) as well as paper or printed format for certification purposes.

Please send the email response to this attorney at: **youremail@ someemailaddress.com.**

SUMMARY

In this chapter we discussed how to obtain call detail records from the wireless telephone companies. We also covered the actual technical language to include in subpoenas for call detail records and also for cell tower location records. The difficulties and directions for obtaining records from opposing counsel were covered and as well as how to determine if you are getting the actual files rather than scanned copies of printed records.

CHAPTER EIGHT

How Cell Phone Location Evidence is Presented in Court

Contents

Introduction   49
    It is all about the maps!   50
    What is the coverage area?   50
    What is radio propagation and how does it look on a map? 53
    The truly odd   55
Summary   57

Abstract

This chapter describes some of the ways that cell phone location evidence is presented in courts. Examples are given of the use of automated tools to create maps that use "standard" radius numbers and how they should be presented; other mapping types are shown which are not based on any real expertise or knowledge. The correct method for use of this information on a map is shown, using open graphics that clearly and precisely illustrate what is known to the analyst/expert in such a case.

Keywords: Cell phone; court; evidence; graphics; maps

Information in this chapter:

- Maps in court.
- Coverage area.
- Radio propagation.
- Presenting the evidence.

INTRODUCTION

Maps showing the results of the analysis of experts and nonexperts is visually compelling and should not be approached nonchalantly. It is critical to understand that the presentation of maps with graphics showing analysis results are powerful and presented incorrectly can be misleading to a jury or judge in a case. In this chapter you are going to see some

Cell Phone Location Evidence for Legal Professionals.
DOI: http://dx.doi.org/10.1016/B978-0-12-809397-9.00008-0

of the many ways that this evidence is presented both improperly and properly.

It is all about the maps!

When an analyst creates maps for use in court, they may attempt to show the coverage area of a cell tower or cell tower sector. Unless they are using radio propagation maps created by a wireless telephone company, any representation of the coverage area of a cell tower sector. There is no way to determine the coverage of a cell tower sector through the use of call detail records. The coverage area of a cell tower is commonly misinterpreted or misrepresented by analysts lacking proper training and or education. In fact, the coverage area of a cell tower should never be part of an analyst's mapping or court presentations unless that information comes directly from the wireless telephone company in the form of a radio propagation map or in some rare cases, in the form of drive testing that occurred contemporaneous to the date and time of the incident. Even then, drive testing has issues that are detailed in Chapter 10, Drive Testing, What It Is and How It Is Used As Evidence.

What is the coverage area?

This is the area around the cell tower where the radio waves reach the ground. This would be the area where a cell phone would be able to successfully make or receive a phone call with good voice quality. This coverage area is often referred to as the radius of the cell tower, or the distance from the tower to the outer edge of the coverage area. Fig. 8.1 illustrates the concept of the radius of a cell tower's coverage area. You see what has been used in many cases to show the "estimated" coverage area of a cell tower, a circle shape divided into three equal pie shaped slices.

This has led many improperly trained or untrained analysts to incorrectly believe that you can use a "standard" radius to show the coverage area of a cell tower. This is incorrect and should never be allowed in front of a jury. Every cell tower and cell tower sector is individually tuned to cover a specific area, and it is common for the sectors on the same cell tower to have different coverage areas. Also, bear in mind as we discussed in previous chapters, cell towers are designed to overlap each other so that the wireless telephone company is providing continuous coverage for their subscribers. No one likes dead zones or dropping calls.

Figure 8.1 Coverage radius with sectors.

The idea behind continuous coverage area is simple: Allow a phone to stay connected to the wireless telephone system when moving around. This requires that there be some overlap of the coverage between cell towers and cell tower sectors. You can think of radio coverage like parking lot lights. Closer to the light pole you have intense brightness. As you move away from one pole, the light becomes less bright. As you enter the area between two lights, you have light from both light poles providing brightness. And finally as you move toward the next light, the brightness increases until you can no longer see any light from another light pole in your immediate vicinity.

Fig. 8.2 shows this concept using the parking lot light example.

Key takeaway: It is not possible to know or determine the coverage area of a cell tower from a call detail record.

The image below demonstrates the difference between an idealized layout of a cell network, and the theoretical service areas of three sectors within the network. (Source: Journal of Digital Investigation, Volume 8, 2012, "Historical cell site analysis—Overview of principles and survey methodologies," Matthew Tart, Iain Brodie, Nicholas Gleed, James Matthews.)

As shown in Fig. 8.3 graphic, cell sectors do not conform to a pie shape. Nor is the coverage area of a circle.

A single cell site (usually a mast or building) can contain the hardware for several cells, which are then also known as sectors. Typically, there will be three

Figure 8.2 Parking lot at night.

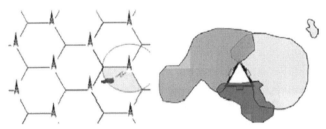

Figure 8.3 Idealized layout of a network (a) and theoretical service areas of three sectors located on the same mast (b).

sectors per cell site and each sector will usually point in a different direction (known as the azimuth) but this can vary, usually between one and six. The sectors will operate independently of each other, having unique cell IDs usually related to each other and similar to the code for the covering cell site. Each sector will provide service over a particular geographical area, and this area will not be uniform (i.e., it will not be a circle, a triangle, or any other regular shape); there may be many different shapes according to geography and the need of the network (e.g., long thin cells on motorways). There may also be disconnected areas of service known as hotspots.

Source: Journal of Digital Investigation, Volume 8, 2012,
"Historical cell site analysis — Overview of principles and survey methodologies",
Matthew Tart, Iain Brodie, Nicholas Gleed, James Matthews.

What is radio propagation and how does it look on a map?

Radio propagation is a term for how radio waves project from a source, in our case a cellular radio antenna, and how those waves act as they spread out from the antenna. Radio waves get weaker as they get farther away from the transmission source, in this case, the radio antenna at a cell site.

Cell tower coverage does not fit into neatly drawn circles or pie shapes. The inherent issue with using maps with circles and pie shapes drawn to illustrate the approximate location of a cell phone is that it gives the incorrect impression, bolstered by expert testimony, that the cell phone location is limited to the area defined by the circle or pie shape. Since it is impossible to determine the distance the phone is from a cell tower at any particular time using the limited data in a historical call detail record, suggesting that the phone is within an arbitrary boundary drawn on a map is inherently false. Fig. 8.4 shows the difference between actual radio coverage and the estimated "pie-slice" method. Note: To the

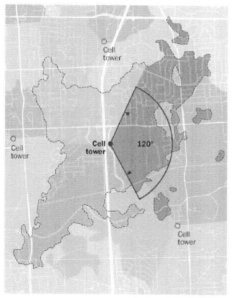

Law enforcement says ...

It is a wedge
Most cell towers have three antennas. Analysts draw coverage areas as wedges radiating 120° from each. They say the range is generally 1–2 miles.

Cellular experts say ...

It is a blob
Phone company coverage maps show that radio waves don't behave uniformly. They can be blocked by topography and other obstacles and can "leak" to areas outside the 120° focus area. Also, the range can vary from a few feet to more than 20 miles.

Also, experts say a cellphone call does not necessarily use the nearest tower, complicating efforts to link a caller to a crime scene. They say that when a phone is in range of more than one tower, an algorithm chooses a tower based on factors such as signal strength, tariffs, and traffic already using that tower.

Sources: FBI Cellular Analysis and Survey Team, Larry Daniel of Guardian Digital Forensics | The Washington Post June 27, 2014

Figure 8.4 Radio coverage infographic. *Source: https://www.washingtonpost.com/local/what-is-a-cell-towers-range/2014/06/27/a41152ce-fe3b-11e3-b1f4-8e77c632c07b_graphic.html.*

best of my knowledge, the FBI is no longer using the pie-slices in their mapping.

Ways that nonexperts show cell phone location evidence in court

No knowledgeable expert in this day and time should be using pie-slices to show cell phone location evidence. The pie-slice originated as a way to show the estimated direction and coverage of cell towers back in the days when templates were used. In the early days of this type of analysis call detail records lacked a great deal of information and in many cases only had the location of the cell tower and nothing else regarding the configuration of the cell towers, that being the information about the sectors and azimuths.

And still today there will be times when the record does not contain complete information about the cell towers, and in those cases, the analyst should not speculate as to the direction of the sector radio antennas.

I see case after case where an "analyst or expert" will use automated tools to create maps of cell towers and sectors that are incorrect. This happens because the person performing the analysis is not doing anything more than loading phone records into a program that does the work and the thinking for them.

These programs are all "law enforcement only" products that are used extensively by nonexperts to produce maps. An example of the output of

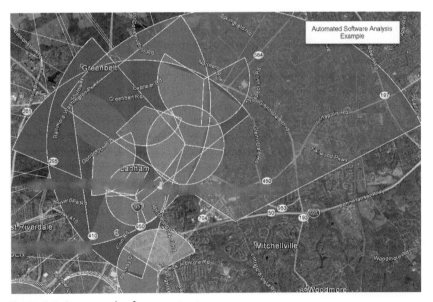

Figure 8.5 Automated software output.

these kinds of programs is shown in Fig. 8.5 where you can see the software draws the pie-slice graphics. The pie-slices are drawn by the software based on the software operator giving the software a radius for the pie-slices. The software then draws the pie-slices on the map. In every case I have seen where analysts have used one of the automated software programs, they give the program a "standard" radius, that is 2 miles or 3 miles. The software will then draw every cell tower the same way. The other issue is that automated software can improperly plot records that should not be used for location purposes or plot records that have incorrect time stamps, or both.

This will result in maps that look like the one in Fig. 8.6. Notice how the cell towers and sectors overlap one another far too much.

The truly odd

There are some truly odd maps that show up in court. The frightening part is that these types of maps are being use to convince juries that the "expert" has some idea of the actual radio coverage of cell towers. Fig. 8.7 shows a map created by a law enforcement officer in a case where based on his training, he thought he could show the coverage of various cell towers by drawing shapes on a map. The shapes on the map are pure speculation based on improper training.

How maps should be presented

The fairest way to illustrate cell phone location evidence is by being clear about what is to be presented. Any map created by an expert or analyst

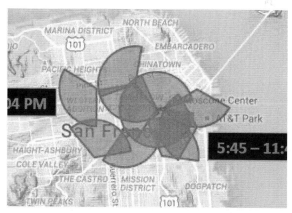

Figure 8.6 Using a "standard" radius.

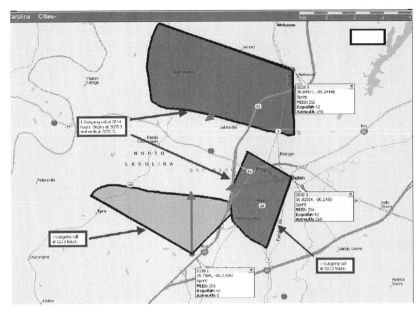

Figure 8.7 A hand drawn coverage map.

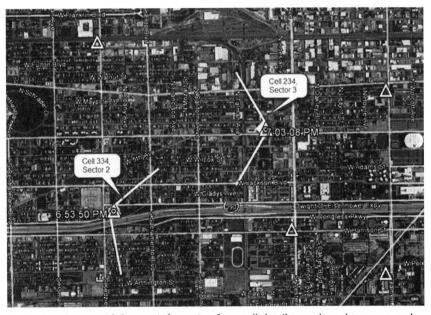

Figure 8.8 A map with known information from call detail records and tower records.

should be based on known factors and should not lead the jury to believe that the expert knows more than is possible from a set of call detail records.

This means that if the expert can determine from the call detail records the direction of the sector radios, that information should be in the map. However, unless there is a radio propagation map or drive testing map that is relevant, no information about radius or coverage should be assumed. Fig. 8.8 shows a map using open graphics to show the direction of radio waves.

Fig. 8.8 shows what can be determined from call detail records and tower records when the information about the towers is available. Each graphic shows the direction of the radio antenna for the respective sectors. No mention is made of coverage area since this information is not known.

An expert would be allowed to opine based on the map in Fig. 8.8 that it would be consistent for the cell phone to be between the two cell towers. However, in that area the cell phone location would be unknown.

Remember, no one ever knows where the cell phone is. The best an expert can do is provide the cell tower locations used by the cell phone and the direction of the sector radio antennas, when known.

SUMMARY

In this chapter, we looked at some of the ways that cell phone location evidence is presented in courts. We also looked at examples of the use of automated tools to create maps that use "standard" radius numbers. Other mapping types were shown that are not based on any kind of real expertise or knowledge. Finally, the proper way to show this information on a map was shown using open graphics that do not overstate what is known to the analyst/expert.

CHAPTER NINE

Issues With Using Call Detail Records for Location Purposes

Contents

Introduction	59
Call Detail Records	60
Data transmission records	60
Text message records	61
Voice call records	61
Experts or not, that is the question	62
Summary	67

Abstract

This chapter discusses how an attempt can be made to locate a phone using call detail records (including call details, data transmission records, etc.) and describes the various obstacles to gaining an accurate location with such an attempt. The various issues that affect cell tower selection by a cell phone are described (such as line of sight, which towers are functioning, radio signal interference, etc.).

Keywords: Call detail records; cell site location information; electronic formats; subpoena language; custodian of records

Information in this chapter:

- Call detail records.
- Location.
- Pings.
- Triangulation.
- GPS.

INTRODUCTION

There are a lot of ways that experts and nonexperts will use call detail records in an attempt to show at best the general location of a phone and at worst claim to know the specific location of a phone.

Cell Phone Location Evidence for Legal Professionals.
DOI: http://dx.doi.org/10.1016/B978-0-12-809397-9.00009-2

Call detail records do not provide a method for precisely locating a cell phone and no claim should be made by anyone to know the specific location of a phone based solely on call detail records, nor should anyone claim to be able to triangulate the location of a phone based on call detail records. In this chapter we will discuss the limitations of using call detail records for locating phones and also the various claims that are made by experts and nonexperts.

CALL DETAIL RECORDS

Call detail records provide information that allows an expert to determine which cell tower was used for a phone call or in some cases, for a text message (AT&T). Call detail records can also contain cell tower information for data transmissions (AT&T) between the cell phone and the network.

While the wireless telephone network does in fact communicate with the cell phone on a constant basis, this does not result in records that are obtainable. These "ping" records are not preserved by the wireless telephone companies for any length of time and are not used as the basis for call detail records.

Data transmission records

Records of data transmissions between the phone and the wireless network are not considered reliable for location purposes and should not be used in the analysis of cell tower locations for a phone.

When you look at the records for data transmissions from AT&T, you can note that the majority of the time stamps are an hour apart. When the transmission actually occurred within that hour is unknown.

The towers used for data transmissions are network directed and the phone can be a long distance from the tower and still show it as a connection when in fact the phone is out of radio range for that tower. I have seen this in many cases where a voice call connection to a phone showing the assumed nearest tower also shows a data connection record for a tower miles away.

Additionally, even when the data transmissions are not being used for location purposes, the fact that a phone is transmitting or receiving data from the wireless telephone network is not dependent on user activity. This means that in the event of an accident potentially involving a distracted driver claim, attempting to determine what the cell phone user was doing at the time cannot be determined from data transmission records.

Text message records

Text message records do not provide a cell tower for the transmission of the texts in a Code Division Multiple Access (CDMA) network (Sprint, Verizon, and so on). In the AT&T network, cell towers that transmitted or received text messages are available. In some rare cases text messages with tower locations may appear in records from other wireless telephone companies, but AT&T is the only carrier that can supply these types of records in just about every case. Call detail records with cell tower information for texts can be treated the same way as voice call records for the purpose of determining the cell tower location that carried the text.

Also, text message records in the call detail records for phone companies will not contain any content of the texts. When the content of text messages is available, it is in a separate data report from the wireless phone company. As a general rule, text message content is not preserved by the wireless telephone companies for more than a few days to a couple of weeks depending on the wireless telephone company and their policies. A good rule of thumb is to always ask them if they still have content. In any event, a preservation letter to the wireless telephone company to prevent the deletion of the text message content can help to preserve the content for analysis. Bear in mind that a preservation letter is not going to bring back messages already purged from the wireless telephone company's databases.

Voice call records

Voice call records are the bread and butter of historical call detail record analysis. It is this information that is used in cases on almost a daily basis now.

With voice call records, as long as the call connects the cell phone to the telephone network, a record is created with the identification of the cell tower and in most cases, the identification of the sector radio set that carried the phone call to or from the phone to the network.

It is the location of the cell tower that an analyst will plot on a map, and if the sector information is known, he or she will also plot the compass direction of the radio waves emanating from the tower.

Experts or not, that is the question

While all of this seems simple on the surface, the danger is that without someone who is an actual expert in how the cellular networks operate and how cell phones interact with those networks, a lay person or an improperly training expert can mislead the trier of fact whether intentionally or unintentionally meaning to do so.

The relationship between cell phones and wireless telephone networks is a complicated one. The following is an excerpt from a declaration I wrote that outlines the factors that must be considered by someone attempting to understand how this works.

Bear in mind that all anyone knows from call detail records is the tower that was recorded in the records, and nothing about why that tower was selected to carry a phone call or transmit a text message. The prevailing opinion among everyone I have seen testify who is an actual expert, is that the phone will connect to the tower with the best signal, and that is "normally" the closest tower. However, bear in mind that there are factors that can be determined that would make that opinion more or less likely and those factors can be considered. For instance, a cell phone on the 25th floor of a building in Manhattan can connect to a cell tower much further away than the closest tower a block away. In fact, in this circumstance, the cell phone might not see the signal from the roof mounted antenna across the street and 20 stories below, and may actually prefer the antenna on a 20 story building a mile away. This can easily change how an expert would interpret the records.

It is important to note that when discussing office buildings in metropolitan areas, the window tint used on modern buildings is often a metalized film that all but blocks the majority of radio signals, including cellular transmissions. The metalized film is what provides infrared heating inside the building, thus lowering their cooling costs significantly. These buildings often are equipped with a distributed antenna system throughout the building that is connected to a high gain directional antenna on the roof that can be pointed to a tower far out of the planned coverage area, for network offloading, traffic balancing, etc.

Cell phones attempt to connect with the tower emitting the strongest and highest quality signal at a given moment, not only the closest. The actual determination of which cell tower is used is complex and hinges on a multitude of factors that are not memorialized in the call detail records.

There is no data in the historical call detail records provided to an analyst that shows why a particular tower was used for a phone call. The analyst must rely solely on the fact that a particular tower was recorded in the call detail records as having been used at the time for the call.

Many factors come into play in the selection of a tower to handle a cellular phone call, and these factors are specific to the moment in time when the call is connected.

Such factors can include:

The loading of the towers in the area, which means, which tower has the available capacity at that moment in time to handle the call.

This is typically the result of a special event, that is a major sporting event, a concert, or other event that would bring more than the normal number of phone users into a specific area. This can also be the result of a natural disaster or even a heavy snow storm where more people are trying to use their phones than would normally be the case for a specific time of day.

The health of the towers in the area at the moment in time, which means, are all towers fully functioning at the time of the call?

The only way to determine if this might have been a factor is to obtain maintenance and outage information from the wireless telephone company. Bear in mind that wireless telephone companies keep a close watch on their towers and will send a crew out very quickly to repair any outage.

The other issue with this is that if a cell tower is recorded as carrying a call, that tower is in operation. Trying to surmise that other towers might be out of service without actually getting that information from the wireless telephone company is just speculation.

Line of sight to the tower from the cellular phone itself. This cannot be determined from just examining call detail records. Other information would have to be available, such as the knowledge that the phone was on the higher floor of a building, or in the subway.

Radio signal interference from other cell towers in the area can also have an impact on cell selection, but it is not something an analyst can determine from call detail records. This can be shown by using a propagation map like the one in Fig. 9.1. In the left side of the map labeled A, I have drawn lines to show the edges of sector 1 for tower 34,016:55,067. The right side of the map B, I have not drawn the lines. The purpose here is to make sure you can see the edges I am describing and then to make this point: Those lines, while they look very defined,

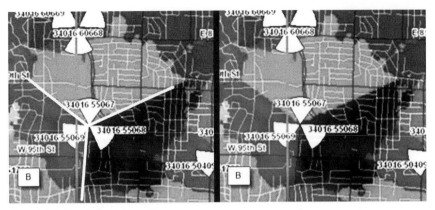

Figure 9.1 Example propagation maps.

are not that precise. In fact, there is an overlap area that is about 10 times the width of the lines I drew in A. This area of overlap is the hand off area between the sectors. As you travel along from northeast to southeast and you leave sector 1, your phone would hand off the call would be handled by the southeastern side of the cell tower noted as 34,016:55,068.

The point of this initial discussion is to show that a phone that starts a call along the edge between the two sectors could select either sector. So while the phone records may indicate that the phone used sector 1, 34,016:55,067 shown in light gray in Fig. 9.1, it could actually be closer to sector 2, 34,016:55,068 shown in black in Fig. 9.1.

In Fig. 9.2, I have highlighted an area using a black box. Within that area you can see several different shades of gray. The purpose of this illustration is to show that radio waves do not form nice clean shapes but tend to run over the radio waves from different towers in the local area. This makes it more difficult to determine which cell tower is in fact the closest cell tower to the phone.

The make, model and condition of the particular cell phone being used can have an impact on how well the phone communicates with cell towers. In fact, even the type of case on the phone can act as a barrier to radio waves.

Fig. 9.3 shows several cell phones that are all on the same wireless network side by side. These phones are all placed together on a table in our forensic lab and placed into engineering mode to show the signal strength

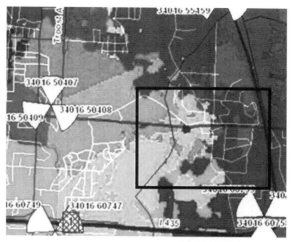

Figure 9.2 Propagation map showing radio coverage overlap.

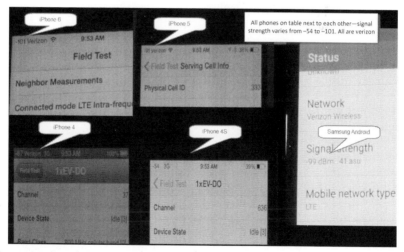

Figure 9.3 Signal strength comparison test.

in numbers rather than bars. As shown in the picture, the signal strengths for the cell towers to the phones vary a great deal.

Multipathing, which is a function of man-made clutter in the area such as buildings and signs that cause radios waves to be reflected. In this scenario a cell phone might be receiving a signal from a cell tower that is broken up into multiple signals that are being reflected to the phone. The ideal is that in a multipath situation, a phone may gather signals from a tower that is not in fact the closest tower to the phone. See Fig. 9.4. It is not possible to determine if this is the case from call detail records.

Another type of fading is called Rician fading. This is created by a knife edge refraction that is formed when radio signals traverse over the corners and roof edges of a building. This can create multipath conditions similar to Rayleigh fading.

If the phone was inside a building at the time the call was recorded, where structural materials may block the signal from one tower, forcing the cell phone to select a different tower than one it would be able to connect with if it were outdoors. Also, if the phone is inside a building with windows that have metal-impregnated glass.

Unusual terrain features such as mountains and valleys, or phones located on high floors of buildings or in basements or subterranean areas such as subways. Without additional information this cannot be determined from call detail records alone. Fig. 9.5 shows some of the ways terrain and other features impact cell phone reception.

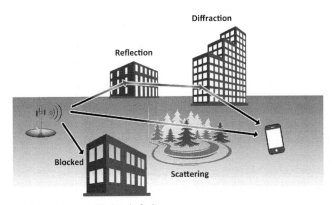

Figure 9.4 Multipathing or Rayleigh fading.

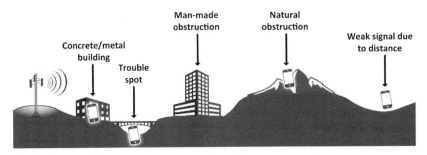

Figure 9.5 Cell reception issues in the real world.

Selection of a servicing cell tower

If a handset is directly in front of, and with line of site to, the antenna for a given cell and with no other cells of greater or equivalent power close by, it would be unlikely to select any other cell.

This means that within the service area of a given cell, there will be regions where a phone could not be reasonably expected to initiate (or respond to) a call on any other cell. The location in question could be termed as the "dominant" region of the cell. Elsewhere, the received signal strength of other cells will be closer to or supersede that of the cell in question. The effects of clutter (either by line of sight, or the effects of localized interference, or "fast fading") will mean that there may be marked differences of signal strength over very many small distances.

If there are other cells serving the area with similar signal strengths, the cell selected as serving by the handset may change frequently.

This (usually much larger) region is termed a "nondominant" area. (Source: Journal of Digital Investigation, Volume 8, 2012, "Historical cell site analysis — Overview of principles and survey methodologies," Matthew Tart, Iain Brodie, Nicholas Gleed, James Matthews.)

A final note on cellular networks is that the coverage areas of the different phone companies are impacted by the cellular band they primarily use.

The areas covered by Verizon, ALLTEL, and US Cellular are predominantly 800 MHz versus those used by Sprint, T-Mobile, Cricket, which predominantly use the Personal Communications Service (PCS) band of 1.9 GHz, which takes on many microwave characteristics, and takes about 2.5 times the number of cells to provide the same coverage. PCS signals can be affected much more significantly by Rayleigh and Rician fading, diffraction, and multipath.

SUMMARY

In this chapter we discussed how an attempt can be made to locate a phone using call detail records and the issues with those attempts. We covered many of the various issues that affect cell tower selection by a cell phone.

CHAPTER TEN

Drive Testing, What It Is, and How It Is Used as Evidence

Contents

Introduction	70
What is Drive Testing?	70
Types of drive tests	71
Drive testing equipment and software	72
Drive Testing Data Collected	73
Drive Testing Methods	74
Drive Test Analysis	74
Drive Testing as Evidence	76
Summary	78

Abstract

This chapter discusses what drive testing is and how some experts will use it as evidence in court. In short, drive testing is a method used by wireless telephone companies and radio frequency engineers to determine the coverage range of a cell tower for the purpose of determining the health of the telephone company's wireless network. Is was not designed for the purpose of establishing an "exact" footprint of the radio coverage of a cell tower sector, nor was it designed for the purpose of establishing the location of a cell phone. Drive testing is also used for the provisioning of new cell towers and for determining where a new cell tower is needed in a network.

Keywords: Cell phone; coverage area; exact footprint; drive testing; radio frequency testing

Information in this chapter:

- Drive testing.
- Types of drive tests.
- Drive testing equipment.
- Drive testing methods.
- Drive testing as evidence.

Cell Phone Location Evidence for Legal Professionals.
DOI: http://dx.doi.org/10.1016/B978-0-12-809397-9.00010-9

INTRODUCTION

Why is this information in a book that is not an engineering manual for radio frequency? Since you as a legal professional will see the results of drive testing in some of your cases you should be prepared to deal with this type of evidence. The maps you will see prepared by experts or radio frequency engineers in cases are the result of the analysis performed. If you are going to use an expert in your case, you will need to obtain the underlying evidence, that is the data collected during the drive test, for your expert to review. You may even decide to test the results of the other side's analysis by having your expert perform an additional drive test.

In other words, you must know that this underlying information exists as part of a drive test and that you can ask for it in the discovery process.

WHAT IS DRIVE TESTING?

Drive testing is a way for wireless telephone companies to get a feel for how the network is perceived by a cell phone user. This analysis of cellular network performance by means of coverage evaluation, system availability, network capacity, network reliability, and call quality is useful to the wireless telephone company. Note that none of the items in the previous sentence include determining the location of a cell phone or setting exact boundaries for where a cell phone must be to connect to a particular cell tower.

When an engineer or nonengineer for that matter decides to perform drive testing, they will gather the testing equipment and software, put it in a vehicle or in a backpack, and then they will go out and drive around to determine the coverage area of a cell tower in an area. Just like any other kind of testing, drive testing results can be skewed by the method used by the person doing the testing. It can also be skewed by whether or not the person doing the testing has had the drive testing equipment calibrated by a qualified calibration engineer. Generally, calibration happens once a year. Equipment that requires annual calibration is tested using measurement technology that is NIST (National Institute for Standards and Technoogy) traceable. By using a cell phone that a subscriber would use, but put into engineering mode for the purpose of drive testing with the mobile phone, the need for calibrated equipment can be circumvented.

Drive testing is primarily a way for a wireless telephone company to get a "feel" for how a user experiences their network when trying to make phone calls. Not all drive testing equipment has the ability to receive calls and the type of equipment typically used in cases does not test the ability of a cellular phone to receive a call at any particular spot in a network. Drive testing equipment can test outgoing call ability by making calls. And some equipment will test incoming call ability by receiving calls. The more common type of drive testing used in cellular analysis cases tests the "listening" signal strength of a unit in idle mode. However, these tests are not performed for the purpose of proving that a phone can make or receive a phone call in a particular place 100% of the time. It is a test to determine if at the time of the drive test and in the location of the drive testing equipment, a phone can make an outgoing call and the phone can "hear" a signal from a cell tower.

Types of drive tests

The main types of drive tests performed by wireless telephone companies are as follows:

1. *Performance analysis*:

    This is the most common type of test performed by wireless telephone companies. Performance analysis testing is usually used to test groups of cell towers called clusters. Performance analysis can also be done to respond to customer complaints about cell phone performance in a particular location.

2. *Integration of new sites, that is determining where a new site is needed*:

    This type of test is performed when a wireless telephone company determines that they may need a new cell site in response to growing customer subscriptions and growing customer complaints in a geographic area. Since the wireless telephone companies must seek municipal approval to install new cell sites, the companies will perform drive testing to show the proposed coverage area of the new sites in relation to existing sites.

3. *Antenna redesign*:

    This type of testing is typically performed by wireless telephone companies for cell sites that are overshooting, that is providing coverage beyond the desired coverage limit for that tower. This can also be performed when a cell sire is undershooting to determine how to re-set the antennas to provide a larger coverage area without overshooting.

4. *Benchmarking*:

This is a test that is used to determine the coverage area of competing networks. You may be familiar with television advertising where Sprint touts being within 1% coverage compared to Verizon. So important is this that the guy who used to work for Verizon whose job it was to go from place to place and call back to Verizon and say, "Can you hear me now?", has now gone to work for Sprint. At least this is the claim in the television commercial. If you read the fine print at the bottom of the television screen, you will see the disclaimer that states that this 1% claim is based on third party drive testing in metropolitan markets. So the claim is not a comparison of coverage for all of Sprint's network to Verizon's network, but is only for limited areas in particular cities. This is where drive testing benchmarking results can be used to solicit new sales. Alternatively, benchmarking can be used to show where a network needs improvement.

5. *Commissioning*:

Drive testing can be used and is used to determine if a newly placed cell site antenna is performing as per design and installation specifications. In this case, prior to the cell site going "live," engineers will use drive testing equipment to determine if the antenna is configured properly to provide coverage in the area where the design engineers predicted where the coverage area would be.

Drive testing equipment and software

Drive test systems are usually built around two measurement components: instrumented phones (test engineering phones) and measurement receivers. There are several companies that manufacture drive testing equipment and software solutions. One of these is JDSU. JDSU is now Viavi Solutions, Inc. Fig. 10.1 is a graphic showing the components in the RANAdvisor from the Viavi Solutions (formally JDSU) company's website technical brochure for the RANAdvisor product (http://www.viavisolutions.com/sites/default/files/technical-library-items/ranadvisor-sg-nsd-tm-ae.pdf).

Another manufacturer is PCTEL, Inc. They manufacture a performance analysis tool called SeeHawk. One member of that product family is SeeHawk Engage Lite shown in Fig. 10.2 from PCTEL's website at http://rfsolutions.pctel.com/content.cgi?id_num = 2166#SHEngageLite.

Figure 10.1 RANAdvisor drive test system for network planning, deployment, and maintenance.

SeeHawk Engage Lite

SeeHawk Engage Lite is an application test tool designed for factory consumer device Quality of Experience (QoE) drive testing and walk testing.

- Application test support
- Software-only solution
- Supports major cellular technologies such as CDMA, EV-DO, GSM, UMTS, and LTE, all in one tool
- Runs on any commercial Android phone or tablet
- Transferrable license allows you to move your software from one device to another with ease
- Powerful real-time visualization of measurement data
- Cloud integration for easy management and file transfer

Figure 10.2 PCTEL's SeeHawk Engage Lite product.

DRIVE TESTING DATA COLLECTED

A large amount of data is collected by the collection hardware/software during a drive test. All of this data is useful in determining exactly what was learned during the test. Some of the dataset collected will be:

Signal strength as measured for the cell sites and sectors within range of the test phone or collection device at each collection point along the drive test route.

Signal quality as measured for the cell sites and sectors within range of the test phone or collection device at each collection point along the drive test route.

Dropped calls as measured during hand-off attempts during connected test phone calls.

Handovers or hand-offs. This is the information about when the phone hands off to a neighboring cell tower or sector while the test phone is connected to the network in a test phone call.

Best serving cell site as measured for the cell sites and sectors within range of the test phone or collection device at each collection point along the drive test route. The best serving cell site is the site with the highest signal strength and best signal quality.

Neighboring cell information as measured for the cell sites and sectors within range of the test phone or collection device at each collection point along the drive test route show those cell sites that are "neighbors" to the cell site that is currently selected by the phone and or the network.

GPS location and coordinates. This is the location of the collection device when it takes a measurement. This allows mapping in conjunction with signal strength and signal quality measurements.

DRIVE TESTING METHODS

Idle: This is a test mode used to record the signal strength and signal quality for cell towers while the phone is in the idle state, that is not making or receiving phone calls.

Dedicated short call: This is mainly used for testing the accessibility of the network. In other words, this tests to see if the phone successfully connects to the network for a phone call.

Dedicated long call: This is mainly used to test the ability of the test phone to maintain a longer phone call with dropping. It is also used to gather hand-off success rates and call drop rates as the test phone moves around in the testing area while being connected to the network for a phone call.

DRIVE TEST ANALYSIS

Analyzing drive test results is more than just taking a screen shot of a map generated by the analysis tool. It should include a review of the collected data to determine that the key performance indicators are examined to make sure that the drive test is a viable representation of the networks interaction with the cell phone used to test the network during the drive test.

Some of the key performance indicators are as follows:

Accessibility: This is a measurement of the call set-up success rate. This is typically viewed as a percentage of calls that were successfully connected to the network. This is measured against the number of connection attempts by the test phone where the number of successful connections is compared to the number of failed connection attempts.

Call sustainability: This is the percentage of calls that dropped during the time when the phone was connected to the network in a test call.

Mobility: This is a measurement of the handover or hand-off success rate that shows the number of times the test phone dropped a call during a hand-off from one cell site or cell site sector to another. A successful handover means that the call stays connected and the handover is transparent to the phone user.

This type of test can show where a network is not functioning properly. For instance, every time I leave my office on Six Forks Road in Raleigh, NC, head south and then turn east on the beltline, any call I have in progress invariably drops. This has been the case for several years and it appears that my wireless telephone company is in no hurry to fix it. No wireless telephone company's network is perfect and they all have holes and weak spots in coverage. What this also means that when a phone should hand-off, but cannot due to holes in the network coverage, the cell phone can "hang on" to the originating tower longer than it is predicted it normally would, effectively "stretching" the coverage of the cell tower.

Radio Frequency coverage: The radio frequency coverage is a measurement of the radio signal strength in a specific geographic area. This may be represented in an expert's report as a map with a coverage area where the collection device or test phone took measurements on the date and time of the drive test. This would not be the exact same measurement that would have been taken on the date and time of the incident (Fig. 10.3).

This can also be represented on a map as a series of dots or other markers of varying colors showing the signal strength at the points where the device took measurements. The purpose of this type of map is to show the best serving cell site and sector for a particular location on the date and at the time of the test. This may not be the same measurement that

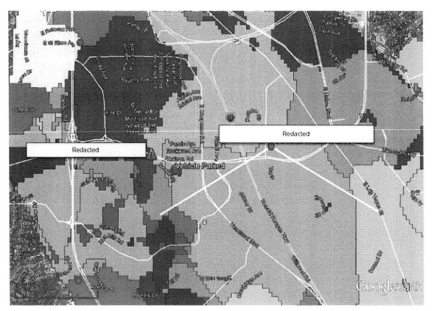

Figure 10.3 Drive test coverage map.

would have been taken on the date and time of the incident. There are so many variables that affect where and when a phone might have coverage from one specific tower or another, that it would be impossible to state that a phone would connect to a particular tower 100% of the time.

DRIVE TESTING AS EVIDENCE

Drive test results may be used in a case to either show that a cell phone could be at a particular place and would prefer the cell site and sector that was recorded in the historical call detail records. Or the drive test results are used to create a map showing the limits of where a cell phone could be and connect to a cell tower or sector.

In the first case, drive test results may be presented as in Fig. 10.4 where dots are shown on a map that purports to be the most preferred cell tower sector for a phone to use.

In the second case the drive test results would be shown as a coverage map that is created like the one shown in Fig. 10.4. This would purport

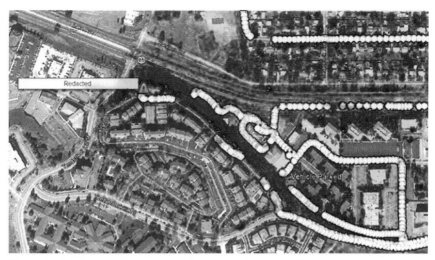

Figure 10.4 Drive test best server points for an isolated cell sector.

to show the limits of where a cell phone could be and connect to a cell tower sector. This may be used in a number of ways to show that a cell phone could be at the location of an incident and receive coverage from a particular cell tower and sector. Alternatively, these kinds of maps can be used to show that a cell phone would have to be in a particular geographic area that would include or exclude a location. For instance, it could be used to show that a person's cell phone could not have been where the person said he was on a particular date and time, thereby eliminating that location for an alibi. Or that the person's phone could have been at the scene of an accident, fire, robbery, murder, or some other incident on the date and time of that incident.

It is critical to understand that drive testing months or even years after an incident is not going to show exactly the same results as a drive test that would have occurred on the date and time of the incident. There are multiple issues with using drive testing as evidence of the proposed limits of where a cell phone could be and connect to a cell tower.

In fact, since radio waves are not static and do not propagate exactly the same way over time, the cell tower and sector a cell phone may "see" or prefer can change even within a few minutes.

Like propagation models, drive tests are limited in their effectiveness because they capture RF propagation characteristics in a given moment of time. Drive tests are more accurate than propagation models but still not the complete answer for predicting how RF signals will propagate at any given time throughout an area. This is because drive tests give an engineer only a snap-shot in time of how RF is propagating from a specific point. It is a physical trait of RF that, at one spot, signal levels could vary greatly at any given moment.

Bedell, Paul. Wireless Crash Course: Third Edition (Kindle Locations 8464–8468). McGraw-Hill. Kindle Edition.

SUMMARY

While drive tests may seem to "prove" that a cell phone must be in a particular area, or that the cell phone would only prefer a particular cell tower and sector, this is not an absolute. As explained in this chapter, examining the underlying data that is the basis for maps presented by experts is a critical step in determining if the map is a true and accurate representation of the data collected during the drive test. Also, bear in mind that a drive test conducted weeks, months, or years after an incident should be suspect since the network can change, individual cell tower configurations can change, and the drive test itself may be flawed. While the expert might contact the wireless telephone company and get an assurance that no significant changes were made in the intervening months between the incident and the drive test, the fact that time has passed can still be a factor as the equipment ages and is subject to maintenance or weather incidents that may have changed the alignment of antennas.

CHAPTER ELEVEN

Per Call Measurement Data—Real Time Tool—Network Event Locations System Data

Contents

Introduction	80
What is "Precision Location" Data?	80
What Are Per Call Measurement Data, Real Time Tool, and Network Event Locations System?	80
Per Call Measurement Data	81
Real Time Tool	83
Network Event Locations System	85
Other factors affecting accuracy	87
Summary	88

Abstract

This chapter deals with what some experts will claim is very accurate methods of locating a cell phone based on "precision location" records. These records are referred to as "network event locations system" from AT&T, "real time tool" from Verizon, or "per call measurement data" from Sprint.

It is critical for you as the reader to understand that none of these methods are historical location data for a cell phone, do not contain accurate GPS locations, and are highly suspect for any kind of use in determining the location of a cell phone other than a general location that is really no more and in many cases less precise than the use of call detail records.

Keywords: PCMD; per call measurement data; real time tool; RTT; NELOS

Information in this chapter:

- Precision location data.
- Location.
- Pings.
- Triangulation.
- GPS.

Cell Phone Location Evidence for Legal Professionals.
DOI: http://dx.doi.org/10.1016/B978-0-12-809397-9.00011-0

INTRODUCTION

This chapter deals with what some experts will claim is very accurate methods of locating a cell phone based on "precision location" records. These records are referred to as "network event locations system" (NELOS) from AT&T, "real time tool" (RTT) from Verizon, or "per call measurement data" (PCMD) from Sprint.

It is critical for you as the reader to understand that none of these methods are historical location data for a cell phone, do not contain accurate GPS locations and are highly suspect for any kind of use for determining the location of a cell phone other than a general location that is really no more and in many cases less precise than the use of call detail records.

WHAT IS "PRECISION LOCATION" DATA?

Many times in subpoenas and warrants you will see a line that is requesting precision location data in the form of PCMD, RTT, or NELOS records. I have even included this request in the subpoena language I provide to attorneys for their use in obtaining call detail records. However, it is important to note that this "precision location data" is in fact no more accurate than a normal call detail record for cell phone location. What it does is provide more data than is available from a call detail record since it contains network activity traffic between a cell phone and a cell tower. Not because there is some magical precise distance from the tower to the phone. And definitely not because there are accurate GPS coordinates in the PCMD, RTT, or NELOS records.

WHAT ARE PER CALL MEASUREMENT DATA, REAL TIME TOOL, AND NETWORK EVENT LOCATIONS SYSTEM?

Each of these tools, PCMD, RTT, and NELOS were created by the wireless telephone companies for the purpose of checking and overseeing their networks.

According to Sprint, PCMD data carries a disclaimer as:

Please be advised that there are known accuracy defects with Sprint PCMD reporting. Therefore Sprint is unable to certify or testify to the accuracy of PCMD records. It is important to understand that the tool used to provide PCMD records was created as a tool for Sprint to oversee the network. It was not created as a tool to identify customer location, pursuant to exigent circumstance, or legal demand. Nevertheless is has been used in those situations as it is a Sprint record that could possibly lead to customer location.

There are several factors that may impact the accuracy of the reporting. Those factors include, but are not limited to, the use of repeaters, small cells, outdated cell records loaded into the tool, and the tool's ability to potentially pick up deactivated devices that have shared the same telephone number.

The latitude and longitude found on PCMD reporting is not historical GPS for the device.

PER CALL MEASUREMENT DATA

PCMD is calculated based on the measurement of the round trip delay (RTD), which is the time the radio signal takes from the cell tower to reach the mobile phone and return. While the speed of radio signals is well known and therefore can be used to measure the distance between a cell tower and a cellular phone, unless the signal is perfectly clean and stable and there is a minimum of three towers in clear line of sight to the cellular phone, the accuracy of the location will be unreliable. There are many factors that can impact the accuracy of these location measurements:

Multi-pathing: Multi-pathing is where a cellular signal is being deflected or otherwise "bounced" from a direction that is not in the direct line of sight between the cellular phone and the cell tower. When this occurs, it is impossible to measure the distance to the tower using RTD as the route is no longer a known factor. A simple way to explain multi-pathing and its effect on RTD time is to think if the radio signal as a ball on a pool table. If the ball is going in a straight line from the cue tip to the rail and back, the RTD can be calculated very accurately. However, if the ball was to be bounced off of a random number of rails prior to completing the round trip back to the cue tip, the distance and time would no longer be a known factor but would be a random amount. This randomness in RTD caused by multi-pathing would cause a major error in the calculation and accuracy of the estimated position of the cellular phone.

Capacity issues: Capacity issues occur when the database computers and processing computers in the cellular network cannot handle all of the data being collected. When this occurs, data is lost. The data that is lost is data from the cell sites that are supposed to be reporting back RTD information for the purpose of calculating the estimated location of the cellular phone. When this data is lost, the system is unable to calculate all of the data associated with the PCMD system and the result is that errors are introduced. However, these errors are not displayed as part of the data provided to law enforcement or anyone else that is attempting to use the estimated locations of the cell phone to show the position of the phone at any point in time. In other words, it is impossible to know when the location information provided for a cellular phone is accurate or inaccurate based on PCMD since the capacity state of the system is not a known factor. For this reason, among others, it is impossible to determine the baseline accuracy of PCMD locations of cell phones or any known margin of error for these estimated locations.

Multiple hand-off connections: A hand-off refers to the process of transferring an ongoing phone call from one cell tower to another cell tower because the phone is moving away from a cell tower, approaching a cell tower, or is in a position where the signal from the cell tower the phone is connected to is not as strong and high quality as the signal from another tower, even when the cell phone is not moving. This occurs when the phone is in a soft-hand-off situation and can be connected to multiple cell towers and cell tower sectors at the same time, making it impossible for the system to determine which towers are to be used in the real time delay measurement. This is because the signal of the best of all the used channels from the towers can be used at any moment or all the signals can be combined to produce a clear signal. This has the same effect on the location measurement as multi-pathing. However, these multiple hand-off situations are not displayed as part of the data provided to law enforcement or anyone else that is attempting to use the estimated locations of the cell phone to show the position of the phone at any point in time. For this reason, among others, it is impossible to determine the baseline accuracy of PCMD locations of cell phones or any known margin of error for these estimated locations.

Repeaters: Sprint and other cellular phone companies employ repeaters in their networks. A repeater is a device that can send and receive cellular signals, but is not local to the cell tower it is using for processing of the signals. It acts like a cell tower, but does not contain the equipment needed to process calls. The repeater takes the radio signal and sends the data over a land line to a cell tower that is being used to process the call. When this occurs, any RTD measurement of the radio signal would be measuring the distance to a repeater station and not an actual cell tower. Since the geographic location of the repeater that is connected to the cell phone is used for the calculation, instead of the location of the actual cell tower the location data is inherently incorrect.

In their European patent application, EP 2 288 200 A1, "Mobile device data collection for use in mobile communications network improvements", Verizon explains in [0004], "Yet another technique for collecting mobile communications network operational parameters is known as per call measurement data method. In this technique, the wireless network communications network takes periodic measurements from the mobile phone and stores them in a central server with a latitude and longitude. This latitude and longitude is determined by using timing triangulation from the cellular towers of the mobile communications network. In such a method, the locations of where the measurements are taken can be very inaccurate due the limitations that result form [sic] timing triangulation. Further, the location of the mobile station can only be determined when the mobile station is seen by a plurality of cellular towers."

REAL TIME TOOL

Verizon, in response to subpoena and warrants requesting data from their RTT, provides the following disclaimer:

The latitude and longitude measurements of the Real Time Tool "RTT" report are derived solely from the Round Trip Delay measurement. They are the best estimates and are not related to any GPS measurement. Measurements with a high degree of confidence factor may be more accurate than measurements with a low confidence factor, but all measurements contained on this report are the best estimates available rather than precise location.

In my experience in dealing with RTT and PCMD data, I have performed data analysis of these types of data in dozens of cases.

The graphic is Fig. 11.1 shows the result of one such analysis where the cell phone was in a fixed location for a period of months. The PCMD data was plotted on a map along with the cell tower location and the cell tower sector information. Considering that the PCMD data is represented in many cases as being very accurate, to within one-tenth of a mile, a study of the data over time shows this to be untrue.

From Fig. 11.1, it is clear that when the location of the cell phone is known and is in a fixed position, the measurements show a wide variation of the cell phones location according to the PCMD measurements. In fact, in this analysis and in every other analysis I have performed using RTT and or PCMD data, the measurements have plotted points behind the antenna set for the cell tower sector which should not be possible. The plot in Fig. 11.1 uses the GPS coordinates in the records to plot the various points. This demonstrates that the GPS coordinates in any of this type of data is unreliable.

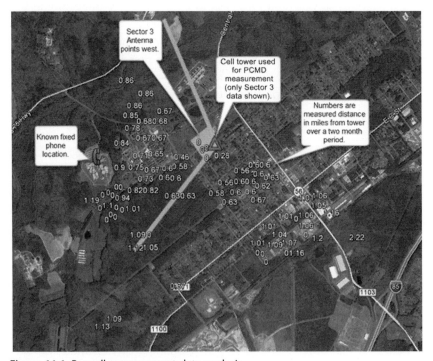

Figure 11.1 Per call measurement data analysis.

When you ignore the data points plotted behind the sector antenna set and only consider the distance measurements in front of the sector antenna, the variation is less pronounced, but still not accurate enough to present to a jury as "precise" location information.

In fact, since it is known that the phone is this example is in a fixed location, note that not one distance measurement is ever at the actual phone location.

This type of data is really no more accurate than simply showing the cell tower sector information, without any of the measurements as the expert can testify to the fact that the cell phone is using the sector antenna set that points in a direction, but cannot testify to the accuracy of any of the points or measurements. And the most critical issue is that no expert outside of someone who is involved in the actual creation of and maintenance of these network measurement tools would be qualified to address the actual accuracy of any of this data. While it is easy to show that the data is inconsistent as an expert who is analyzing the records, it is not so easy to prove that this is scientifically reliable enough to proclaim that the location of the cell phone is known at any point.

The issue with showing this type of analysis to a jury of laypersons is that it gives more credence to claims of knowing the location of a call phone by both experts and nonexperts who are simply plotting locations on a map using this flawed data.

NETWORK EVENT LOCATIONS SYSTEM

NELOS is a tool used by AT&T to oversee their network.

On every page of their NELOS reports, the following disclaimer is present:

The results provided are AT&T's best estimate of the location of the target number. Please exercise caution in using these records for investigative purposes as location data is sourced from various databases which may cause location results to be less than exact.

In a motion in limine to exclude NELOS data from being used in a case, the attorney argued that the state must demonstrate that the procedures AT&T used to gather and to process the data on which the state's expert's report was based would satisfy the reliability standards of the Ohio Evidence Rule 702(C).

Some excerpts from the motion are included here:

NELOS (i.e., the Network Event Location System) is a recently invented technology. It purports to locate a cell phone that cannot be located through use of GPS technology. NELOS technology is the subject of several patents belonging to AT&T Mobility II LLC.4.

The first NELOS patent was apparently issued on July 17, 2012. A second patent was issued about a year later, and the third a year after that, on November 11, 2014. A number of other patents appear closely associated with the core NELOS technology.

The most recent patent that that appears to relate to NELOS technology was issued on January 20, 2015.

According to the patents, the NELOS technology purports to locate a cell phone by contemporaneously recording certain information that has been transmitted in packets of electromagnetic pulses. The pulses are transmitted to and from an AT&T customer's cell phone or other electronic device. The transmissions are with whatever number of AT&T's cellular towers that are within range. NELOS purports to use these exchanges of information — and, most importantly, their timing — to approximate the cell phone's location when the device cannot be located by GPS technology.

Electromagnetic pulses travel at the speed of light. In a vacuum, light travels at 186,000 miles per second. That equates to nearly 300,000,000 meters per second. To put that speed in perspective, the circumference of the earth is a bit less than 25,000 miles. A pulse of light traveling in a vacuum would, therefore, circumnavigate the earth 7.5 times in one second.

The pulses tracked in the NELOS technology do not, of course, travel in a vacuum. The speed at which an electromagnetic pulse is travels outside a vacuum is affected by delays that are associated with the various media through which the pulse passes. The principal media affecting NELOS technology are those in the user's cell phone or device itself, in the various components of AT&T's communications network that are involved in the communication exchanges, the geographic distances over which the communications occur, and the local atmosphere in which they all exist.

Using clocks that are in the user's device and in AT&T's various network components, NELOS purports to measure the minuscule differences in the time it takes the pulses to travel between the user's cell phone and the various towers communicating with it. NELOS then calculates the time-differentials between when the pulse was sent and when it was received. After adjusting for delays caused by the various media through which the pulses have passed, NELOS plugs the computed duration of the various exchanges into a variety of formulae which then purportedly calculate the location of the user's device. Obviously, the reliability of the NELOS procedure depends, in very large part, on calculations of the tiny differentials that the NELOS technology purports to measure and record. It also depends upon the accuracy and precision of the various clocks that mark the moments when the various propagations and transmissions begin and end.

NELOS technology purports to be capable in some circumstances of detecting the location of a cell phone to within 25 meters. For NELOS to achieve that order of accuracy, it must consistently detect and record time-differentials with extreme accuracy. In any system that measures and compares geographic distances by measuring time-differentials of electromagnetic pulses that travel over various distances, a discrepancy of even a fraction of a millisecond would produce a potentially discrediting error. For example, an error of one one-hundred-thousandth (.00001) of a second can mean an error of almost two-miles (186,000 + × .00001 = 1.86 + miles). So, to have any relevance to the facts of this case, the State must demonstrate that

- *each detection of pulses*
- *at each location that is relevant in the NELOS system,*
- *each calculation that quantifies the time-differentials,*
- *the entire algorithms that processes that information, and*
- *the clocks that each of these steps depends on*

consistently and accurately functioned at levels that produce the degree of precision that the NELOS report presumes.

Defendant has no way of knowing whether the NELOS procedure is reliable enough to produce results with the accuracy that would make the NELOS report relevant to the distances that will be at issue in this case. Because AT&T's patented technology is subject to trade-secret protection, the Defendant has been unable to locate any peer assessments of the NELOS technology or other validation of the specific algorithms it employs.[13] And because the NELOS technology is so new, no reported cases have yet examined whether the NELOS procedure satisfies the requirements of Evid. R. 702(C).

Other factors affecting accuracy

One thing we have not discussed is installation error, or sector reversals. While the phone company will use its known published engineering data to release to subpoenas, on occasion there are physical anomalies that can negate the information delivered.

While cellular carriers make every realistic attempt to test and verify antenna connections are correct for each sector, mistakes can be made anywhere humans are involved, and the sheer number of towers, antennas, tower crews, and base stations raises the probability of physical engineering errors to a level of probability over mere possibility.

Physical hardware problems can be situations such as:

1. Antennas are not connected to the correct inputs on the base station.
2. Antenna jumpers may not be connected in the correct sequence, and it is possible for a call to appear on a sector different from where it actually was.

3. Maintenance personnel testing or repairing cell sites, on rare occasion, may not re-connect antennas to the proper base station inputs.
4. Tower crews replacing, changing, or moving antennas, on occasion, may get the connections at the top of the tower out of sequence.
5. New installations improperly installed, due to any variety of factors, and not fully verified by knowledgeable system quality personnel.
6. Antenna azimuths are not pointed as engineered. While a site will still work fairly well, the major radiation pattern will have shifted off of where it is expected to cover.

A friend of mine who works for law enforcement related a story to me about a case he was involved in where the call detail records did not match the story of one of the victim witnesses. The call detail records, if correct, made it impossible for the victim to be where she said she was at the time of an abduction of a family member.

As it turned out, when he performed drive testing, he determined that the call detail record was incorrect because the radio frequency measurements showed a different coverage area than was reported.

Once he got an engineer involved from the wireless telephone company, it was discovered that someone had connected the wires backwards for one of the sector antennas, effectively making the equipment show that the antennas pointed in a different direction than what was reported via the call detail records.

An important takeaway here is that once again, it is important to understand that the wireless telephone system is designed to provide wireless phone service, not to locate people. This condition in the network could have continued for years without notice by the phone company since they do not care where a phone is, only that they are not receiving complaints about availability or "coverage."

SUMMARY

In this chapter, the three types of "precision location" data were described and discussed in some detail as to how the data is collected and some of the issues with the data for location of cell phones. We learned that PCMD and RTT data is not as accurate as it may appear to be upon casual inspection. We also learned that NELOS data suffers from the same type of inaccuracies in the recording of the data and the calculation of the location of the cell phone.

CHAPTER TWELVE

Emergency 911 System

Contents

911 Wireless Services   90
   911 wireless services   90
   Unique challenges posed by wireless phones   90
   Tips for 911 calling   90
   Ask about your handset's enhanced 911 capabilities   91
   Improving wireless 911 rules   92
   Compliance   92
Enhanced 911 Wireless Location Services   93
The Enhanced 911 System Overview   93
Location Technology   95
The Future of Enhanced 911   97
Tracking a Phone Using Enhanced 911   97
Summary   98
References   98

Abstract

One of the more accurate ways of determining the location of a cell phone is through the activation of the Enhanced 911 (E911) emergency system. The Federal Communications Commission requires that wireless telephone companies be able to locate a cell phone when that phone dials 911 independent of any GPS capability within the cell phone itself. In this chapter we will discuss the E911 system and how it can be used to locate a cell phone.

Keywords: Cell phone; E911; emergency system; GPS; location; ping; tracking

Information in this chapter:

- Enhanced 911 wireless location services.
- FCC rules.
- Pinging.
- Public safety access point (PSAP).

Cell Phone Location Evidence for Legal Professionals.
DOI: http://dx.doi.org/10.1016/B978-0-12-809397-9.00012-2

The cellular system was not designed to determine the physical location of cellular phones. Cellular mobile phone networks are optimized for capacity and call handling, not for location of cellular phones. From the standpoint of the cellular provider, there is no value added in being able to locate a cell phone, and hence no reason to invest in that type of technology. However, the Federal Communications Commission (FCC), which governs the wireless and wired telephone industry, requires that each of the wireless telephone companies be able to locate a cell phone in the event of an emergency.

911 WIRELESS SERVICES

The following is from the FCC's website [1]:

911 wireless services

The number of 911 calls placed by people using wireless phones has significantly increased in recent years. It is estimated that about 70% of 911 calls are placed from wireless phones, and that percentage is growing. For many Americans, the ability to call 911 for help in an emergency is one of the main reasons they own a wireless phone.

Unique challenges posed by wireless phones

While wireless phones can be an important public safety tool, they also create unique challenges for emergency response personnel and wireless service providers. Since wireless phones are mobile, they are not associated with one fixed location or address. While the location of the cell site closest to the 911 caller may provide a general indication of the caller's location, that information is not always specific enough for rescue personnel to deliver assistance to the caller quickly.

Tips for 911 calling

Consumers making a 911 call from a wireless phone should remember the following:
• Tell the emergency operator the location of the emergency right away.

- Provide the emergency operator with your wireless phone number, so if the call gets disconnected, the emergency operator can call you back.
- Public safety access points (PSAPs) currently lack the technical capability to receive texts, photos, and videos.
- If your wireless phone is not "initialized" (meaning you do not have a contract for service with a wireless service provider), and your emergency call gets disconnected, you must call the emergency operator back because the operator does not have your telephone number and cannot contact you.
- To help public safety personnel allocate emergency resources, learn and use the designated number in your state for highway accidents or other nonlife-threatening incidents. (States often reserve specific numbers for these types of incidents. For example, "#77" is the number used for highway accidents in Virginia.)
- Refrain from programming your phone to automatically dial 911 when one button, such as the "9" key, is pressed. Unintentional wireless 911 calls, which often occur when auto-dial keys are inadvertently pressed, cause problems for emergency call centers.
- If your wireless phone came pre-programmed with the auto-dial 911 feature already turned on, turn this feature off (consult your user manual for instructions).
- Lock your keypad when you are not using your wireless phone to help prevent accidental calls to 911.
- Consider creating a contact in your wireless phone's memory with the name "ICE" (In Case of Emergency), which lists the phone numbers of people you want to have notified in an emergency.

Ask about your handset's enhanced 911 capabilities

When replacing your handset, ask about E911 capabilities. Some providers may offer incentives to encourage customers without location-capable phones to obtain new location-capable phones. Some providers may choose to prevent reactivation of older handsets that do not have E911 capability, or they may adopt various other measures. If a provider declines to reactivate a handset that is not location-capable, the FCC still requires the provider to deliver a 911 call from that handset to the appropriate PSAP.

Improving wireless 911 rules

The FCC has adopted rules aimed at improving the reliability of wireless 911 services and the accuracy of the location information transmitted with a wireless 911 call, as part of our efforts to improve public safety. The improvements help providing PSAPs with meaningful, accurate location information from wireless 911 callers in order to dispatch local emergency responders to the correct location and to provide assistance to 911 callers more quickly.

The FCC's wireless 911 rules apply to all wireless licensees, broadband personal communications service licensees, and certain specialized mobile radio licensees. Mobile satellite service providers, however, are currently excluded.

The FCC's basic 911 rules require wireless service providers to transmit all 911 calls to a PSAP, regardless of whether the caller subscribes to the provider's service or not.

Phase I E911 rules require wireless service providers to provide the PSAP with the telephone number of the originator of a wireless 911 call and the location of the cell site or base station transmitting the call.

Phase II E911 rules require wireless service providers to provide more precise location information to PSAPs; specifically, the latitude and longitude of the caller. This information must be accurate to within 50−300 m depending upon the type of location technology used.

The FCC recently required wireless carriers to provide more precise location information to PSAPs. As a result, wireless carriers will be required to comply with the FCC's location accuracy rules at either a county-based or PSAP-based geographic level. The new standards apply to outdoor measurements only, as indoor use poses unique obstacles.

Compliance

Wireless service providers are required to file with the FCC a list of counties, or portions of counties, that they seek to exclude from the location accuracy requirements. The FCC permits exclusions only where wireless carriers determine that providing location accuracy is limited, or technologically impossible, because of either heavy forestation or the inability to triangulate a caller's location. Wireless carriers must report any changes to their exclusion lists within 30 days of such changes. The exclusion lists and changes must be reported in the record of the FCC's docketed proceeding addressing location accuracy, PS Docket No. 07–114, which is publicly available online.

ENHANCED 911 WIRELESS LOCATION SERVICES

With the development of the E911 system, it is possible to locate a cell phone with varying degrees of accuracy and success depending on the level of E911 services available in the locality.

Phase I E911 location is limited to just the cell site location and in some cases the sector antenna of the cell site. This is provided at geo-location coordinates (latitude and longitude) of the cell. In some rural areas where small wireless telephone companies operate, or very remote areas like the everglades, parts of the major mountain ranges, swamps, large national park areas, and some other locales, it is not possible to provide a precise location for a cell phone based just on triangulation of cell towers. In these Phase 1 areas, the location of the cell phone can be miles away from the location of the cell tower.

Phase II E911 location requires the wireless telephone company be able to provide to the emergency operator that the PSAP both the cell site information and the geo-location of the actual cell phone. In a Phase II system, the accuracy of the location is required to be between 50 and 300 m. The accuracy that the technology can achieve is dependent on several factors. One of which is the length of the 911 call. Calls that last less than 45 seconds do not provide the system enough time to perform additional location calculations. In these cases the accuracy can be much less than 300 m. One of the reasons is that the emergency dispatcher can ask the system to update the location measurement for the caller by performing a "re-bid" of the 911 location system. This will provide the dispatcher with an updated and usually more accurate location for the cell phone.

THE ENHANCED 911 SYSTEM OVERVIEW

The purpose of the E911 system is to provide geo-location information to emergency services personnel when a caller dials 911. With the advent of wireless technology, a system had to be implemented that could handle the location of a wireless caller.

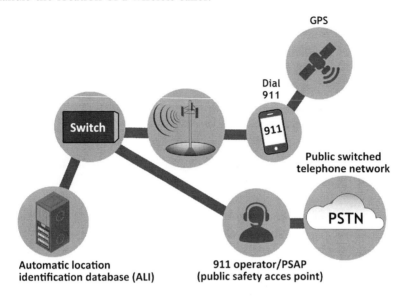

However, the reality is that the 911 system is not fully implemented in all areas due to several factors, including geographic considerations and lack of cell towers that would make accurate location of a cell phone impossible. If the 911 call is a Phase 1 call, all the wireless carrier is required to provide the calling number and the location of the cell tower. This means that the call location can be anywhere in the overall sector of the cell tower coverage area.

In fact, one of the key factors in gaining a more precise location of a cell phone is the length of time the phone is connected to the PSAP's emergency operator. If the phone call to the 911 operator lasts less than 45 seconds, the system does not have time to update the location of the cell phone. This location updating is called "bidding." Once the operator and the caller are in the call for more than 30 seconds, the operator can re-bid or request a location update. This will provide in many cases, a more precise location of the cell phone.

If the phone call terminates prior to the re-bid, the cell phone location will not be as accurate and may be limited to only knowing the geolocation of the cell tower that carried the 911 call to the PSAP.

In extreme rural areas, the lack of cell towers can make it impossible to locate a phone more accurately than within several square miles. This is because in order for the cell phone to be located the system must have more than one tower in communication with the phone to "triangulate" its position. When the phone cannot communicate with more than a single cell tower, triangulation is impossible.

LOCATION TECHNOLOGY

There are more than one way to locate a cell phone, triangulation using cell site locations and the use of the GPS chip that is embedded in the majority of modern cell phones today.

The first type of location technology is called radiolocation and is dependent on using multiple cell site locations to determine the location of the phone by a method known as time difference of arrival (TDOA) (Fig. 12.1).

TDOA works on the basis of the amount of time it takes for a radio signal from a cell site to reach and return from a cell phone, and then the difference is calculated for that measurement for several cell sites that can communicate with the cell phone. For example, if the cell phone can communicate with three or more cell sites, then the different amounts of time are measured and then the system will calculate the distance from the cell site location to the cell phone. Once all of the distances are known, the system will "triangulate" the location of the phone with some degree of accuracy.

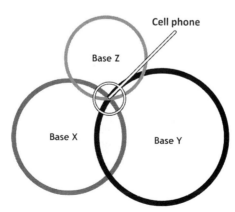

Figure 12.1 Time difference of arrival.

Another method is call angle of arrival (AOA). In AOA, the time and distance calculations are based on only two cell sites. Then the point where they meet is used to estimate the location of the cell phone (Fig. 12.2).

Finally, there is handset-based location technology. This uses the GPS chip that is present in most cell phones today to retrieve the GPS location from the cell phone. This is possible with cell phones that have the E911 location feature. The E911 location feature in cell phones allows the phone to send its location to the PSAP.

Nearly all major wireless telephone companies today (Verizon, Sprint, AT&T, T-Mobile, US Cellular to name a few) have the ability to use the GPS chip in the phone for location services. However, the location accuracy of the GPS chip in the phone is greatly reduced inside buildings and in dense urban environments.

This is because the 911 system was developed specifically for emergency services over the last 20 years. And that process that resulted in a system that works best outdoors where cell phones have a clear view of the sky for phone-based GPS location and a clear view of multiple cell towers for network-based location.

The system as it stands today does not use the location-based services (LBS) developed over the last few years by commercial interests. This is why Uber can locate you when E911 cannot. This is also why when someone calls 911 from their cell phone the dispatcher will always ask for your location. If you can give a physical street address or a set of cross streets, the dispatcher can relay that information to first responders.

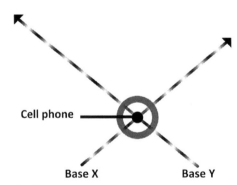

Figure 12.2 Angle of arrival.

THE FUTURE OF ENHANCED 911

The E911 system is working now to adapt new technologies that will assist in locating cell phones more accurately both inside and outside of buildings. The E911 system is also implementing text-to-911 location services as well.

As the E911 system adapts to using LBS, as well as using wireless access points, the ability for the system to accurately locate a phone will improve dramatically. Additionally, applications that use voice over internet protocol (VOIP) have been a problem for E911 call centers because they do not use the traditional wireless telephone system like a phone call would. This prevents the E911 system from locating the cell phone. However, new advances in working with VOIP calls is now being adapted by the E911 system so that a caller using SKYPE or another VOIP application can be located by the E911 system [2].

TRACKING A PHONE USING ENHANCED 911

When law enforcement personnel want to know the location of a cell phone, they can request the wireless telephone company to activate the E911 system for a phone number.

At that point, the E911 system will start to "ping" the phone about every 15 minutes. At that point, if the cell phone is turned on, the system will obtain a location for the phone just like it would if that person had dialed 911 on their cell phone.

This location data is sent to an email address provided by the law enforcement officer who requested the E911 activation.

Law enforcement can obtain E911 tracking in multiple ways, including a request under exigent circumstances, which can start the tracking immediately pending a follow up warrant to the wireless telephone company. A missing person, alleged kidnaping, danger to an individual or to the public are all considered exigent circumstances for the purpose of activating the E911 system.

Another way for law enforcement personnel to obtain location data using the E911 system is through a warrant or a "trap and trace" order. These methods normally require a warrant signed by a judge or magistrate and are required to meet the same standards for other types of warrants.

SUMMARY

In this chapter we discussed the E911 location service for wireless telephones. The challenges wireless phones pose to 911 emergency services were discussed. The current and emerging technologies for locating cell phones via the E911 service were discussed as well and the methods used by law enforcement to obtain E911 location information for the purpose of locating and tracking a cell phone.

REFERENCES

[1] FCC.GOV, (2016) 911 Wireless Services. [online] Available at: https://www.fcc.gov/consumers/guides/911-wireless-services [Accessed December 12, 2016].
[2] ctia.org, (2016) Mobile 9-1-1 Calls Explained. [online] Available at: http://sf8.dmz.ctia.org/policy-initiatives/technology-topics/mobile-9-1-1-calls-explained   [Accessed December 12, 2016].

INDEX

Note: Page numbers followed by "*f*" refer to figures.

A

Accessibility, 75
Accuracy, factors affecting, 87–88
Accuracy of the location, 30, 93
Airplane mode, 5
Antenna beam widths, 16
Antenna redesign, 71
AT&T, 21, 46, 60–61
   data transmissions from, 60
AT&T records, 38, 39*f*
Automated tools, 54
Automatic roaming, 38
Autonomous registration, 21
Azimuth, 14, 38

B

Base station controllers (BSCs), 18–20
Base transceiver station (BTS), 10, 11*f*,
      18–19
Beamwidth, 14
Benchmarking, 72
Best serving cell site, 74
Bidding, 94

C

Call angle of arrival (AOA), 96, 96*f*
Call attempt, 27
Call capacity of the cell tower, 14
Call detail records, 30–31, 33, 41–42,
      60–67, 80, 88
   business purpose for, 34–35
   code division multiple access (CDMA)
         network records, 36
   data transmission records, 60–61
   global system for mobile
         communications network records,
         36–39
   issues to be aware of in reading, 38
   issues with, 59
   obtaining, 41–42

   cell tower records, 46–47
      from opposing party, 45–47
   origination, 34–39
   proof of a service provided, 35
   requesting, 43–45
   selection of servicing cell tower, 67
   technical picture of each transaction, 35
   text message records, 61
   transaction record for financial
         accounting purposes, 35
   type of data in, 35–36
   voice call records, 61
Call sustainability, 75
Called historical cell site location
      information, 33–34
Capacity issues, 82
Cell hawk, 54*f*
Cell phone, 1–5
   common misconceptions, 5–6
   smart phones, 2–3
   working mechanism, 4–5
      in wireless system, 23–25
Cell phone call
   anatomy of, 26
   cell phone to cell phone call, 26*f*
   hand offs, 27–28
   land line phone calling a cell phone, 26*f*
   types of, 27–28
Cell phone location, working of, 29–31
Cell phone location evidence, in court, 49
   coverage area, 50–52
   maps, 50
   nonexperts showing, 54–55
   radio propagation, 53–55
   truly odd maps, 55–57
      presentation, 55–57
Cell reception issues in the real world, 66*f*
Cell site location information, 34–35
Cell sites, 8–10, 11*f*, 16, 18–19, 19*f*
   mounted inside a billboard, 9*f*
   mounted on top of a water tower, 10*f*

Cell tower identifiers, 36–38
Cell tower lists, 43–46
Cell tower location records, 41–42
Cell tower records, 46–47
Cell towers, 5, 7, 16, 18–19
    capacity, 12–13
    co-location, 14–16
    configuration, 13
    coverage area, 50
    covering a long highway, 14f
    sector towers, 13–14
    three sector configuration, 15f
    with zero sectors, 13
Cellular networks in urban and suburban
        areas, 16
Cellular repeaters, 19
Cellular system, anatomy of, 20f
Clusters, 71
Code division multiple access (CDMA)
        network records, 21–22, 25, 36
Commissioning, 72
Communications Assistance to Law
        Enforcement Act, 46
Completed call, 27
Coverage area, 50–52, 70
Coverage radius with sectors,
        51f

D
Data transmission records, 60–61
Dedicated long call, 74
Dedicated short call, 74
Dialed digits, 36
Difference of arrival, 95f
Digital subscriber line (DSL), 18
Directional antenna beam widths, 16
Distributed antenna systems (DAS),
        16
Drive testing, 31, 69–72
    analysis, 74–76
    data collection, 73–74
    equipment and software, 72
    as evidence, 76–78
    methods, 74
    performance indicators, 75
    types, 71–72
Dropped calls, 74

E
Enhanced 911 (E911) emergency system,
        30–31, 89
    compliance, 92–93
    future of, 97
    handset's enhanced 911 capabilities, 91
    improving wireless 911 rules, 92
    location technology, 95–96
    911 calling, tips for, 90–91
    911 wireless services, 90
    overview, 93–95
    tracking a phone using, 97–98
    unique challenges posed by wireless
        phones, 90
    wireless location services, 93
Enhanced Node B, 10
Ericsson switches, 38
Everglades, 5

F
Federal Communications Commission
        (FCC), 89–90, 92–93
    wireless 911 rules, 92
Fiber distributed data interface (FDDI), 18
Flip phone, 2
Forwarded call, 27
4G systems, 10

G
Global positioning system (GPS)
        coordinates, 31
Global system for mobile communication
        (GSM), 21–22, 25
Global system for mobile communications
        network records, 36–39
GPS chip, 5, 96
GPS location and coordinates, 74
Graphics, 51–53

H
Hand offs, 25, 27–28, 28f, 74, 82
Handovers, 74
Handset's enhanced 911 capabilities, 91
Handset-based location technology, 96
High-speed digital communications lines,
        18

Historical cell site location information, 33–34
Home location register (HLR), 18, 21, 23–24, 24f

I
I-85 North, 10
Idealized layout of a network, 52f
Idle, 74
Integrated digital services network (ISDN), 18
Integrated media server (IMS), 26
Integration of new sites, 71
International mobile equipment identifier (IMEI), 21
International mobile subscriber identifier (IMSI), 21
ISP list, 42, 43f

J
JDSU, 72

L
LAC/NEID, 45
Law enforcement, 30–31, 97
"Law enforcement only" products, 54–55
Location registers and roaming, 21–22
Location-based services (LBS), 96
Lucent switches, 38

M
Maps, 49–50
  presentation, 55–57
Memory buffer, 26
Mobile switching centers (MSCs), 18, 26, 34
Mobile telephone switching office (MTSO), 19–20
Mobility, 75
Multipathing, 65–66, 66f, 81–82
Multiple hand-off connections, 82

N
Network equipment identifier (NEID), 36

Network event locations system (NELOS), 31, 80, 85–88
911 calling, tips for, 90–91
911 wireless services, 90
  compliance, 92–93
  handset's enhanced 911 capabilities, 91
  improving wireless 911 rules, 92
  911 calling, tips for, 90–91
  unique challenges posed by wireless phones, 90
NIST, 70
Non-POTS technology, 18
Nortel, 38

O
Ohio Evidence Rule 702(C), 85
Omnidirectional antennas, 19
Omnidirectional towers, 13

P
PCS signals, 67
PCTEL, Inc., 72
Per call measurement data (PCMD), 31, 79, 84f
  factors affecting accuracy, 87–88
  network event locations system, 80–81, 85–88
  per call measurement data, 81–83
  "precision location" data, 80
  real time tool, 80–81, 83–85
Performance analysis, 71
Phase I E911 location, 93
Phase II E911 location, 93
Physical hardware problems, 87–88
Pie-slices, 53–55
Pings, 31, 60
Plain old telephone system (POTS), 17–18
"Precision location" data, 80
"Precision location" records, 80
PREPS (Pilot Reports), 25
Propagation maps, 64f, 65f
PSTN, 26
Public safety access points (PSAPs), 91–92

R

Radio channels, 4
Radio coverage infographic, 53f
Radio Frequency coverage, 75
Radio network controller (RNC), 19
Radio propagation, 53−55
Radio propagation maps, 50
Radio signal interference, 63−64
Radiolocation, 95
Radius of the cell tower, 50
RANAdvisor drive test system, 72, 73f
Rayleigh fading, 65−66, 66f
Real time tool (RTT), 31, 80, 83−85
Real-time data collection, 31
Real-time geo-location tracking, 31
Receiver radio, 4
Registered phone, 24−25
Registration process, 23−24
Repeaters, 19, 83
Repoll number, 36
Rician fading, 66
Roaming, 21−22
Round trip delay (RTD), 81−83
Routed call, 27

S

Search.org
   home page, 42f
   ISP list dropdown, 43f
SeeHawk, 72
SeeHawk Engage Lite, 72, 73f
Servicing cell tower, selection of, 67
Signal quality, 74
Signal strength, 65f, 67, 73
SKYPE, 97
Smart phones, 2−3, 3f
Sprint, 21−22, 36, 72
Sprint call detail record example, 37f
Sprint phone, 23−24
Standard cell phone, 2, 3f
"Standard" radius numbers, 57
Subpoena language, 41−43, 45

Subpoena requests, 41−42
Subscriber-specific information,
   maintaining, 21
Switch network equipment identifier,
   36
Switches, concept of, 34

T

Text message records, 61
360° coverage area, 13
Three sector cell tower, 13−14
Time difference of arrival (TDOA), 95
T-Mobile, 46
Tracking, 5, 97−98
Transaction record for financial accounting
   purposes, 35
Transmission radio channel, 4
Transmitter radio, 4
Triangulation, 31, 83
Truly odd maps, 55−57

V

Verizon network, 8−10, 21−22, 36, 72,
   83
Viavi Solutions, Inc., 72
Visitor location register (VLR), 18, 21
Voice call records, 61
Voice over internet protocol (VOIP), 26,
   97
Voicemail, 27

W

Wireless 911 rules, improving, 92
Wireless system, working of cell phones in,
   23−25
Wireless telephone company, 5−6, 30, 36,
   45
Wireless telephone network, 4−6, 17−20,
   20f, 34, 60
   location registers and roaming, 21−22
Working mechanism of cell phone, 4−5